BREAK POINT

BREAK POINT

TWO MINNESOTA ATHLETES
AND THE ROAD TO TITLE IX

SHERI BRENDEN

UNIVERSITY OF MINNESOTA PRESS
Minneapolis — London

The University of Minnesota Press gratefully acknowledges the generous assistance provided for the publication of this book by the Margaret S. Harding Memorial Endowment, honoring the first director of the University of Minnesota Press.

Royalties from the sale of this book are donated to the Tucker Center for Research on Girls and Women in Sport at the University of Minnesota.

Published by the University of Minnesota Press
111 Third Avenue South, Suite 290
Minneapolis, MN 55401-2520
http://www.upress.umn.edu

ISBN 978-1-5179-1458-5 (pb)

A Cataloging-in-Publication record for this book is available from the Library of Congress.

Printed in the United States of America on acid-free paper

The University of Minnesota is an equal-opportunity educator and employer.

30 29 28 27 26 25 24 23 22   10 9 8 7 6 5 4 3 2 1

To Peggy and Toni, who refused to be sidelined

CONTENTS

PROLOGUE

This is the story of two athletes and their shared legacy.

It is not about breaking records or claiming championships. No, this is a story of two high school girls with a passion for sport who believed they should have the same opportunities as boys to learn, train, and compete. They pressed on even as they were told they didn't belong, they weren't good enough, they would hurt boys' athletic experiences and undermine girls' opportunities.

This story is about more than sports. It is about a historic court decision on gender equity that launched a movement among girls and women and put educational institutions on notice: they could no longer stall or ignore gender equity in athletics.

Part of this history occurred in my community of St. Cloud, Minnesota. I saw it through adolescent eyes at our kitchen table. It appeared in the newspapers, played out in the courts, and was the subject of much debate. This slice of history includes play-by-play coverage from athletic contests and attorney strategies from federal courtrooms.

At its heart, this is a story about two girls who did not think they should have to wait for equality.

In the early 1970s, few girls imagined themselves as athletes, schools barely budgeted for girls' sports, and state tournaments and college scholarships were intended for boys. The starring roles were always male; females were cast as "adoring fan," "pretty girlfriend," or "perky cheerleader." We all knew the familiar plotline: Boy joins team. Boy encounters and overcomes obstacles. Boy wins championship thanks to courage, hard work, team spirit, and support from coach and community. Everyone loves that story!

"Historically, what it meant to be an athlete was the same thing as what it meant to be male. In contrast, what it meant to be female traditionally was the antithesis of being an athlete," says Mary Jo Kane, founder of the Tucker Center for Research on Girls and Women in Sport at the University of Minnesota.[1] "We were told for genera-tions that the reason that girls and women didn't play sports is be-cause it was preordained, biologically, physiologically."

"There was just absolutely no thought that institutions should put any resources into women's sports," Kane adds. "In the 1970s, the Minneapolis park board spent more money on boys' hockey sticks than on the entire girls' program combined." Colleges didn't offer any athletic scholarships to women. "The prevailing attitude was girls aren't interested in sports. And even if they were, they wouldn't be any good. Why make the investment? Girls aren't supposed to play sports."

All that changed on May 1, 1972, when Judge Miles W. Lord is-sued a federal court decision that opened the door for two Minne-sota girls from public schools in St. Cloud and Hopkins, Minne-sota to compete on their high school athletic teams. With the help of the Minnesota Civil Liberties Union, Peggy Brenden and Toni St. Pierre—one a tennis player, the other an endurance athlete who ran and skied cross-country—had sought the opportunity to train and compete head to head against other high school athletes. Previ-ously, their schools offered only a smattering of sports options for girls and forbade girls from competing with boys.

The U.S. District Court for the District of Minnesota points to the decision as one of its eight most significant cases.[2] Upon appeal, it was upheld by the Eighth Circuit Court of Appeals, establishing a legal precedent that pressed schools across the country to create sports participation opportunities for girls. In addition, the Eighth Circuit panel pointed out that Title IX, a relatively new civil-rights law enacted to protect women's access to educational opportuni-ties, should be interpreted to include athletics. Even though Title IX doesn't specifically mention sports, the court declared that inter-scholastic athletics were an important educational opportunity, and "discrimination in high school athletics constitutes discrimination in education."[3]

The case unlocked the gates to an arena that had been constructed with only one gender in mind. Girls everywhere who had once stood on the sidelines started to see themselves racing to a finish line, scoring a crucial point, or claiming a victory. My interest in this history is especially keen because it involves my sister. Almost six years older than I am, Peggy Brenden is the benchmark by which I measure my actions. She's the compass I use to calibrate my path, my possibilities. I've had my eye on her since I was born. And because she is my sister, I witnessed her part in this history as it happened on the tennis court, in our house, and at school. I was watching from a front-row seat. But being only twelve years old at the time, I confess I missed plenty: the media coverage, the legal arguments, the conflicting reactions, and the many people involved. As an adolescent, so many big events seemed to be sprinting through my life—junior high dances, puberty, a federal court case, painting my bedroom—it was impossible to sort it all out.

Decades passed before I even attempted to examine the people and events surrounding the federal court decision that carries the Brenden family name. Lacking a childhood diary or old letters chronicling personal reflections and family dynamics from the time, I started by paging through Peggy's fragile scrapbook held together with tape, yarn, and paper clips, a collection of brittle news articles, typewritten letters, and lighthearted narrative. Peggy created this A-B-C, step-by-step guide titled "How to Play High School Tennis—An Instructional Manual." The scrapbook begins "A. Have a very supportive family" and ends with "Q. You may find the debate team is a less stressful alternative."

Armed with this cache of primary documents, I tapped into research skills I had honed as a librarian, writer, and reporter. I combed through old newspapers, reviewed court transcripts, and interviewed coaches, attorneys, and a legendary federal court judge. I tracked down high school teammates and opponents, traveling to Phoenix, Kansas City, and many other places to conduct interviews. I scrolled through reels of old newspapers on microfilm and negotiated document requests from the National Archives and Records Administration. Much of the story came right from my own backyard, from people who lived in Minnesota, some only a few miles away. More important, most of them were quite eager to help, telling their part of the story.

Toni St. Pierre, the other plaintiff in the case along with my sister, grew up in the same community where I now live, and she attended the Hopkins public school system as my own children did. Diagnosed with a rare form of cancer while training for the Boston Marathon, Toni died in 2013. I was never able to meet her or talk to her, but she left a trail that I have uncovered—of newspaper articles, team records, and recollections from her coaches, teammates, and family that reveal a girl who was both passionate and driven.

Break Point tells the story of these two teenage girls and their 1972 lawsuit. It is based on historical records, legal documents, and the voices of people who both supported and opposed them. While it is not a memoir, it is colored by my own passion for sport and gender equality. I tell this story as a sister who admires Peggy and Toni, as an athlete who celebrates their impact, and as a woman who cares about their legacy. These two trailblazers confronted and battled sexism that was, and still is, all too common in sports. As teenage girls, they found their paths were obstructed by many layers of resistance; their talents and skills were disrespected; their opportunities were limited; and their narratives were marginalized. But despite living in an era when girls' ideas, skills, and dreams were subordinate to those of boys, Peggy Brenden and Toni St. Pierre stepped forward and refused to be ignored. In claiming their identities as athletes, they opened a door for girls everywhere.

1

THE LETTER

Peggy Brenden and Toni St. Pierre wanted nothing more than the same opportunity their male classmates had come to expect for decades: to be part of their high school sports teams—teams with coaching, practices, teammates, opponents, uniforms and competitive events. They wanted their share of the "wide world of sports," a chance to train hard, build skills, and experience "the thrill of victory and the agony of defeat."[1]

But simply asking wouldn't be enough. Neither tenacity nor talent would assure either a place in a team lineup. It would take the weight of the U.S. Constitution and a 1972 federal court decision to allow the addition of their names to rosters filled with boys.

The first shot across the bow in this battle rang through the Brenden house with a penetrating *ding*. The sound would have spilled down the stairway and nudged me, Peggy's little sister—slightly. But I mostly ignored what was happening. Our black Underwood typewriter resided upstairs and was known to make that *ding*. I recognized the thump that followed when a typist shoved the carriage return back to start a new line. Perched on an old sewing-machine table in the upstairs hallway, the typewriter was at the ready for anyone who cared to pound out a few keystrokes.

Typing was a skill our mother encouraged. She considered it an important career competency, especially for her daughters. Nursing, teaching, cosmetology, and clerical work were the primary career paths available to women at the time, and our mother had used her typing skills when she had been employed long before I was born. I often called on her help when I needed an important letter or paper typed quickly and professionally. She had nimble, strong fingers and could speed up and down the keys.

Peggy didn't rely on anyone else to compose or type her letter that day in October 1971. She tackled the task herself. A high school senior, she had learned to type in summer school and could rival anyone in words per minute. Her fingers flew. After drafting the letter in pencil and carefully checking punctuation and spelling, Peggy began banging the keys, striking them with authority. The message had to be right, not full of Wite-Out—it needed to look clean and read clearly. She addressed her urgent plea for help to the Minnesota Civil Liberties Union (MCLU).[2] Then Peggy sealed the envelope, licked the stamp, and put the letter in the mailbox.

That same fall, Toni St. Pierre was putting in roadwork around Hopkins, a small suburb of Minneapolis. A junior at Hopkins Eisenhower High School, she followed a training schedule that included running long distances with the boys on the school cross-country team and racing in shorter Amateur Athletic Union (AAU) events against other girls. Toni's feet were callused and hard. She liked to run through parks and golf courses barefoot, feeling the grass and soil with each step. Her technique was distinctive: her upper body flowed smoothly while her legs remained almost stiff, making her easy to spot in a pack. During her workouts, she chatted and laughed easily with her companions. But come race time, she was intensely competitive. Quiet and withdrawn before putting her toes to the starting line, she was focused, intent on making sure all her early-morning runs and extra miles paid off with a better time, a better finish. Though her stride was a bit choppy, Toni's commitment to her training never wavered.

"She had a tough, tough attitude," said Patrick Lanin, a distance runner and coach at Hopkins Eisenhower.[3] He believed it was her grit and determination that set her apart. He told the *Pioneer Press* in 1972, "Toni's real talent is in her mental and emotional attitude . . . Toni never quits. She always keeps going."[4]

"Her training was really important to her," said her younger brother Sam St. Pierre. "It didn't matter to her what the weather was like; she would go out and run. If she had to run at night, my grandfather would follow her in the car." Toni would urge her grandfather to turn on the music and open the windows, accompanying her as she ran.

Lanin, who was Toni's AAU coach, challenged and encouraged her. He also included her in his team training. Lanin had a knack for fostering an infectious camaraderie.

"Pat Lanin set the tone," said Gary Lee, who both skied and ran on Lanin's teams. "He was somebody who loved the sport, loved to coach people, and was willing to help anybody and everybody."

Lanin had started a cross-country program at the local junior high in 1967, was president of the Minnesota Association of the AAU, and would serve as a Hopkins high school coach for three decades. He and his wife, Emily, became legendary among distance runners and skiers for their role in starting the Minnesota Road Runners Club,[5] organizing and running numerous races, and coaching four Olympians.[6] Their energy and enthusiasm helped motivate countless budding athletes.

When he was hired as the Eisenhower High School coach, Lanin made a point to introduce Toni to the boys on his team and invite her to work out with them. A young, wiry distance runner, he prided himself on developing new runners. He was the kind of coach who would give students used running shoes, who would call to alert them of upcoming races and urge them to participate. Though he had high expectations for his athletes, Lanin allowed them to run to the beat of their own drummer. Often, he ran alongside them. At practice, the team ran in small packs, chatting and joking, depending on the intensity of the workout. No one trained alone.

"He wanted you to train hard and run hard, and he also wanted you to understand that you could have fun running cross-country," said Tim Heisel, who was shy and introverted as a high schooler. When Lanin suggested Tim and Toni run together in the off-season, a strong training partnership was born.[7] As a senior and sophomore, respectively, they ran in an AAU mixed doubles relay cross-country event at Minnehaha Park, winning the 5-mile race with a margin of over a minute.[8] Toni had the fastest girls' time with 7:15 for a mile and a quarter. Logging miles in tandem became central to their teenage social life. Tim and Toni dated some in high school, attended nearby colleges, and married in 1975. The couple had three children before divorcing in 1985.

Eisenhower's cross-country teams prided themselves on being different, wacky, edgy. Until the Minnesota State High School League (MSHSL) put the kibosh on it, the runners usually competed barefoot, pounding over dirt paths and grassy hills. They loved the feel of the ground under their toes and were convinced their feet were lighter and quicker sans shoes. (Besides, shoe technology hadn't yet evolved to deliver the light, cushioned footwear runners craved.)

Outside practice, team members banded together to create "Ike's Army," an offbeat cheer squad that sat together at football games dressed in army fatigues or helmets, leading their own chants to rouse the crowd. At a time when high school coaches were often known for toughness and drill-sergeant discipline, Lanin brought a counterculture vibe. Several team members had long hair, and others had beards and mustaches—the type of grooming many coaches forbade. But Lanin, who wore a mustache and hair over his collar himself, had no rules about personal grooming. He was comfortable with the team's appearance and helped cultivate the quirky sense of pride its members took in their yearbook photo. They didn't pose in uniform on the bleachers. Instead, Lanin's crew loved to cook up unusual locations and attire. They would use their runs to scout out backdrops like a boarded-up farmhouse or railroad trestle. Then they threw in strange props like broken tricycles and pickaxes.

"We were just goofy," said Lee, who posed shirtless in one team photograph wearing swim briefs beneath a towel with boots and a hardhat. The picture was shot outdoors in the snow.

Heisel characterized himself and his teammates as "dorks" or "nerds." It was a shared identity, a team identity. They knew they were considered weird, so including someone who was even weirder than they were—an outgoing, rebellious girl who wanted to run—was just fine.

The Eisenhower cross-country team became Toni's crew. Teammates were known to hang out at her house and run by her side. Together, they covered long distances, starting the season at 4 to 5 miles and working their way up to 10 to 12. Lanin believed in building a long-distance base and doing speed workouts once or twice a week. He would provide running plans to guide his athletes and expected them to put in the roadwork. Toni fell in step. She ran at 5 a.m. She ran when it was freezing. She assaulted hills, pounded pavement, and wove through the woods.

Though she matched the boys stride for stride, she was always an outsider at race time: she could not participate as a competitor in the team's dual, triangular, or invitational meets because she was a girl. Her teammates joked that she should just put on a stocking cap and run in the team races.[9] As an athlete who wanted to stretch and challenge herself, Toni knew she needed race experience to push and motivate her. "It's not just that I want to compete on boys' teams, though the equal rights aspect is part of it. It is mostly that I want good competition so I can improve in my sports," she said in 1972.[10]

Peggy faced the same obstacle in central Minnesota, where she attended St. Cloud Technical High School, better known as Tech. As a junior, she asked the school tennis coach, Bill Ritchie, whether she could play on his team. Ritchie, a large man with short-cropped black hair, had recently returned from Vietnam and had just landed a job as both math teacher and tennis coach for the 1970–71 school year. In the latter role, he followed Mac Doane, a local legend who had served as the school's head tennis coach for thirty-one years until moving to the city's new high school, Apollo. Coach Ritchie's response did not give Peggy much encouragement. No, he couldn't allow it, he told her. It was prohibited by Minnesota State High School League rules. But he did let her practice with the team—sometimes, anyway, when there was an odd number of boys. After school each day, Peggy changed into shorts and a T-shirt and headed to the tennis courts, hoping for a chance to play. Occasionally, she got to step in as a practice partner, but some days she just walked home or hit tennis balls against the wall by herself.

It wasn't enough. And she could see it wasn't going to change before she graduated. In the fall of her senior year, St. Cloud Tech organized extramural tennis for girls, which amounted to organized play days with no instruction or coaching. It drew a small group of players, most of them new to the game. They were rained out more than once.

One fall afternoon, after their usual tennis workout, our older sister Sandy and her husband, Jim Tool, began talking to Peggy about a girl who attended a St. Paul junior high. Kathryn Striebel was trying to swim on the Murray High School boys' team—there was, of course, no girls' team. Peggy was not alone in searching for a chance to play and compete. Maybe they didn't attend her school, but there were other girls who wanted the chance to build their athletic skills, share team camaraderie, and compete fiercely. And some of them weren't taking no for an answer.

Jim, a junior high assistant principal, had recently taken an education law class in which he had heard about cases initiated by the American Civil Liberties Union (ACLU), a nonprofit organization that advocates for individual rights. Unlike my parents, Jim loved to passionately debate politics and boldly voice his positions on issues. He casually suggested that Peggy seek the help of the ACLU. "The only reason she didn't have an opportunity to play was because she was a girl," Jim said. "I kind of thought the Civil Liberties Union would take the case."

Peggy needed no prodding. She took this offhand suggestion and turned it into a plan of action. It offered both a spark of hope and a path forward. "It started me thinking: maybe my disappointment wasn't unique to me," Peggy recalled. "Maybe the unfairness I was experiencing was potentially big enough to interest the MCLU, an organization that could bring about real change; maybe I didn't have to accept the way things were. Sandy and Jim's nudge made me believe change was possible and that I could help make it happen."[11]

Our parents' position seemed to be subtly supportive. They never attempted to dissuade Peggy from pressing her case, but they also never made calls to the school board or demanded action from coaches and school administrators. Peggy's tennis game was not "their" issue. Our mother did not consider herself a feminist. She was a capable and hardworking woman, a homemaker who seldom discussed politics. She didn't go to political protests or sign petitions.

But she did recognize that her child had a passion and a talent for tennis. She could see that there were coaches, opponents, travel, and training for boys who cared half as much about playing the game as Peggy did. Why shouldn't she enjoy the same opportunities?

Still, our mother and father didn't actively encourage Peggy to challenge the rule keeping her off the boys' team. Rather, they chose not to discourage her. Peggy said she sensed our father's pride when people asked him about the case. Yet he did not offer pep talks or trumpet her accomplishments. Our parents simply took Peggy's goals seriously. For Peggy, that felt like unflagging support.

She sent her letter to a local branch of the MCLU. The organization had established a presence in St. Cloud in September 1971 when it announced a newly appointed chairwoman and a sixteen-member committee. It would serve as an investigative body for the state headquarters in Minneapolis and focus on issues related to academic freedom and civil liberties in high schools and elementary schools. Voter registration, especially for college students, was of particular interest.[12]

That fall, Yvonne Hartz, the MCLU St. Cloud chairwoman, alerted the organization about a local voter registration system that required women to fill out a form that was color-coded and labeled "women" with questions about marital status. Men were not required to answer such questions.[13] It's hard to know why the city of St. Cloud wanted that information or how it intended to use it.

In the 1970s, St. Cloud, which was later named an All-American City by the National Civic League, was similar to many cities across the country. It had felt the rumblings of civil rights activists and feminists but remained somewhat insulated from that change and determined to hold on to certain traditions and values. Located in the center of the state, St. Cloud is just 65 miles from Minneapolis, Minnesota's urban hub. Despite this proximity, it felt closer to cornfields and quarries when I was growing up. News from Minneapolis and St. Paul—which in our neck of the woods were known as "the Cities"—was far away and largely unrelated to our world. St. Cloud, with its population of nearly forty thousand, had its own major institutions: a state college and two Catholic colleges nearby, a regional hospital, a daily newspaper, a prison, a large shopping mall, and a veterans hospital. The Mississippi River flowed through the heart of the city, only a half mile from the Brenden house. Surrounded by farms and tiny towns, we were proud of all our city had to offer, and we were suspicious of big-city wealth and lifestyles.

Oh, sure, we were missing a few things. We didn't have a professional sports team; the St. Cloud Rox, a farm team of the Minnesota Twins, folded in 1971. But our family still watched plenty of athletic action. Our father consumed a steady diet of pro baseball and football games on television. Raised on a farm in tiny Starbuck, Minnesota, where he attended class in a one-room schoolhouse, Dad didn't have athletic traditions in his past but was still fascinated by sport. At nearby Halenbeck Hall, we watched the St. Cloud State Huskies men's basketball team and cheered especially fiercely for a star guard who rented one of our bedrooms for college housing. We brought our blankets and sat in the bleachers at Selke Field, surrounded by trademark granite walls, to watch Huskies football. We attended lots of high school games. All of the competitors were male; the fans never considered the possibility of rooting for female athletes.

Our community lived by conservative values when it came to gender. In the 1970s, a banker wouldn't give a loan to a woman without her husband's signature, even if she earned higher wages. The newspaper referred to a woman by her husband's name—Mrs. John Doe. The county clerk, Genevieve Sand, was aghast at the prospect of a married woman keeping her birth name. "I just don't know how we could change our index system without a terrific legal mix-up," she protested in 1972.[14]

Combining men and women in the same activities or spaces was often taboo, regardless of age. At the junior high school, hallways near the locker rooms were designated girls only and boys only. At the high school, there were separate teachers' lounges for men and for women. In seventh grade, girls were required to take home economics; boys took industrial arts. There wasn't a choice. This was our world when Peggy addressed her letter to the newly formed MCLU in St. Cloud. Some of the people on that committee would certainly have recognized her name, as a few members were St. Cloud State College pro-fessors, and we practically lived on campus, surrounded by students and teachers in the houses and apartments of our Southside neighborhood. Both Peggy and I attended the Thomas J. Gray Campus Laboratory School, just a few blocks from our house. In fact, Peggy went all the way through the ninth grade at the college-run school.

Campus Lab, as it was called, was a school where teachers used cutting-edge educational concepts and college students studying to be educators could gain classroom experience from master teachers. As students, we trained rats to run through mazes; created interactive environments of light, wind, texture, and darkness in art class; operated power drills and lathes to build cribbage boards; and were introduced to fencing, folk dancing, and trampoline jumping. It was a public school with no tuition fees. Peggy and I flourished in this learning environment, along with many of our neighbors who also attended. It felt like a neighborhood school, but students came from all over the city. Our teachers were affiliated with the college, and many classmates were children of college faculty members.

Peggy didn't really know what to expect from her letter. She knew our family didn't have an attorney or the money to hire one, but often the MCLU was able to resolve issues simply by writing a letter or making a call. Perhaps that's all it would take to give her a chance to play tennis. Perhaps she could find somebody who could overrule the rule, somebody who understood how much she wanted to play the game.

St. Cloud Tech's athletic director, George Potter, didn't understand. A former football, basketball, and baseball coach, he didn't even bother to raise the matter with the school principal after Peggy asked. Potter's attention tended to focus only on "major" sports, like those he coached, and he wasn't known for providing much support to "minor" ones, like tennis. And he really didn't have time for Peggy. In his mind, it was clear-cut: girls couldn't play on a boys' team. "The official position of the school is the position of the High School League," Potter told the student newspaper at the time. "The rule is that boys and girls aren't allowed to compete."[15]

Like every other public school in Minnesota, St. Cloud Tech belonged to the Minnesota State High School League, which governed sports teams, sports teams, and fine arts competitions. A team that defied MSHSL rules, which were strictly enforced, lost its eligibility. That meant no games, no record, and no tournaments for anyone on the school's team. So no one dared defy the rules for fear of ruining their boys' sports season.

The league first took shape back in 1901, when St. Cloud superintendent Waite A. Shoemaker became one of the key proponents in establishing some controls over high school athletics. Educators were concerned with eligibility issues and "win-at-all-costs" philosophies. For example, should a pupil who had attended school for less than two weeks be able to compete on a school team?[16] While the MSHSL governed all sorts of extracurricular school activities, its roots were firmly planted in boys' athletics.

Still, as early as 1891, Minnesota schools, small and large, had their own girls' basketball teams—there were nearly two hundred in the state by the early 1920s.[17] In fact, nationwide, thirty-seven states held girls' state high school basketball tournaments in 1925.[18] But in only fifteen years, those teams all but disappeared. An organization called the National Amateur Athletic Federation (NAAF), formally organized in 1924, was created in response to concerns about the lack of fitness in the United States and the "perception that competitive sports for girls and women had developed unacceptable practices and abuses." The NAAF Women's Division studied athletic programs for girls and women and set standards.[19]

The NAAF recommendations became guiding principles for women's athletics over the next several decades. Enjoyment, rather than winning, was the focus. The proper motivation for competition was "play for play's sake" as opposed to prizes and individual achievements. Uniforms needed to sufficiently cover girls' bodies, and players were discouraged from participating in athletic competitions against other schools and institutions. An acrimonious debate emerged over the appropriate nature of female competition. Athletic leaders warned that highly competitive sports like track and field and basketball were harmful and would result in the loss of "womanly" qualities.[20]

Female athletes across the country were told their participation in athletic competition was exploitive and unfeminine. They heard warnings about the detrimental effects of intense physical activity on their health. Schools were advised to replace girls' teams with recreation programs. Many high schools organized Girls Athletic Associations (GAA), which offered swimming lessons, after-school games, and "play days" with other schools. Interscholastic teams were dropped. The schools' stated focus was on inclusion, but there were not nearly as many girls in GAA as there were boys in interscholastic athletics.

In Minnesota, it wasn't until 1968 that the MSHSL adopted a resolution to take on administering girls' interscholastic programs. The league adopted bylaws for girls' athletics the following year,[21] including a rule that explicitly forbade mixed-gender athletics. Previously, only some sports had explicit rules against boys and girls competing. Now, there would be no exceptions: "Girls shall be prohibited from participation in the boys' interscholastic athletic program either as a member of the boys' team or a member of the girls' team playing the boys' team. The girls' team shall not accept male members."[22]

The "philosophy and guidelines" for the girls' rules included a unique statement regarding interscholastic athletics, noting that they were "designed to serve the highly skilled girl" without hurting existing girls' athletic programs. Some physical educators believed that boys' sports teams disproportionately served elite athletes and did not want girls' programs to use a similar model.[23]

The creation of bylaws for girls' athletics signaled an interest in creating girls' interscholastic teams, but schools moved at a snail's pace. The January 1971 edition of the MSHSL *Bulletin* reported only forty-seven schools had registered their intent to conduct one or more girls' interscholastic programs,[24] and registration did not mean a school actually had a team in place. The league recommended that school districts first develop strong intramural and extramural programs for girls in various sports, allocating a "reasonable share of facilities, budget and personnel."[25] Then, as facilities, coaches, and interest all intersected, they could introduce interscholastic athletics.

Some high schools offered intramural programs in which girls would play games within the same school or in extramural competition. According to the 1971–72 MSHSL handbook, these programs were "for girls who would enjoy an occasional, sometimes spontaneously arranged, contest with girls from another school." A school was restricted to three such events per intramural sports season. In contrast, interscholastic athletics included coaching, practices, and multiple scheduled contests with teams from other schools.

Minnesota institutions showed little urgency as they considered providing athletic opportunities for girls. While boys' sports were embraced and cheered, many people were unsure that girls belonged on school teams. Were competitive sports really appropriate for girls? In a 1971 Connecticut Superior Court case, a sophomore girl, Susan Hollander, wanted to run with the boys' cross-country team. The judge just didn't see the point: "Athletic competition builds character in our boys," he stated. "We do not need that kind of character in our girls, the women of tomorrow."[26] Rather than focusing on legal issues, the judge's comments regarding the failed lawsuit reflected common attitudes of the time. He believed a girl competing with boys would diminish the sport, her femininity, and the boys' motivation and performance. Regulations separating competition by gender were necessary, he claimed, to maintain the custom and tradition of sport and prevent participants from psychological harm.[27]

MSHSL's Dorothy McIntyre would be forced to confront those attitudes over and over. Her job was to grow girls' athletics. "I was hired in 1970 to help schools develop teams," said McIntyre, who helped craft the girls' athletics bylaws.[28] She was given primary responsibility for managing girls' interscholastic athletics. As a physical education and social studies teacher in the early 1960s, she had worked with colleagues to develop gymnastics clinics across the state, which drew hundreds of girls.[29] It is worth noting that when McIntyre began her duties, the MSHSL board praised her patience, rather than her advocacy, stating, "We believe she will be patient and understanding in our attempt to find the proper place for girls in the competitive sports program at the same time being extremely careful to preserve and ever improve girls physical education, intramurals and extramurals."[30]

McIntyre could see there was a long way to go in building girls' programs: "The landscape was still pretty bare with a scattering of school teams experimenting with some competition in various sports around the state. So we continued working, expanding our efforts and encouraging schools to develop teams as quickly as they could."[31]

School leaders contended they were not in a position to provide the money and facilities required to serve girls. "Imagine you're an athletic director in a high school with all these programs for boys, and in come the girls with a program that could be as big," McIntyre said in 1972. She could see that coaches feared the dollars used for boys' teams would be reallocated to fund girls' teams. "I don't think in the next few years anybody's going to split a budget down the middle—because the interest of boys (in sports) is still higher that the interest of girls."[32]

For the 1971–72 school year, participation figures showed 171,509 boys competing in fourteen MSHSL-sponsored activities. Football, the most popular, claimed 44,800 participants, while curling, a recent addition in 1969, had 312 participants. Baseball and track were available in more than 428 of 484 high schools. Cross-country running, golf, and wrestling were offered in more than half of Minnesota schools. A Minnesota boy could typically expect to choose from seven or eight interscholastic teams at his high school.

The Minnesota Department of Education counted girls' participation differently combining extramural and interscholastic programs for a total of 46,003 girls participating in five sports: track and field, basketball, volleyball, gymnastics and swimming.[33] Although the MSHSL handbook listed twenty-one "approved activities" for girls' interscholastic competition, ranging from archery and badminton to speedway and speedball, most of those sports were not offered to any Minnesota girls. (Some of them, like speedway, were never widely played or even recognized.) Fewer than one hundred high schools provided even one or two girls' interscholastic teams. Track and field and basketball had the most participation. There were only four Minnesota schools that sponsored as many as five interscholastic girls' teams.[34]

Minnesota's school districts were committed to funding athletic programs for their male students, but for girls, not so much. For example, in one of the state's largest school districts, Minneapolis, the athletic budget for the 1971–72 school year was about $212,900, of which $12,800 was allotted to girls' interscholastic sports. Salaries totaled $302,000 for boys' coaches and $21,000 for girls' coaches.[35] Four years earlier, the girls' program received no money at all.

At St. Cloud Tech during the same school year, the boys' athletic budget was $26,000, and there was no budget for girls' sports. Any expenses related to girls' athletic activities were paid with funds intended for physical education classes.[36] Tech boys played more than a dozen matches during the spring tennis season, and the team had court time for daily practices, two paid coaches, a volunteer coach, and a match schedule of over two months with travel to places as far as Moorhead and White Bear Lake, Minnesota.[37] The team could participate in sectional, regional, and state tournaments organized by the MSHSL, which had been held since 1950.[38] Meanwhile, the Tech girls were offered an extramural program in the fall that included a chance to play against one another once a week after school over the course of a month.

The fabric of high school life was woven around supporting the local boys on the football field or basketball court and reading accounts of their athletic exploits in the hometown newspaper. I regularly joined the Friday-evening ritual of attending Tech's football games, chasing my friends around on the grass behind the cement stadium seats. High school girls could participate as part of the pep band, the high-kicking Tigerette dance line, or the cheerleading squad, chanting catchy rhythms about our "Tiger Machine." Even boys like my brother, Jerry, a slim debater who had only a marginal interest in sports, played football at St. Cloud Tech. It was expected.

Jerry was the oldest child in our family. My parents had five children over the course of twenty years. The oldest three siblings (Jerry, Judy, and Sandy) were bunched together, born in 1939, 1941, and 1943. Both Jerry (class of 1957) and Judy (class of 1959) graduated from high school before I was born. Peggy arrived in 1954, and I came in 1959.

While Peggy and I shared a bedroom and bathroom for a time,

she eventually moved to new digs in the basement after our parents finished a fourth bedroom there—though "finished" is a rather loose term for the remodeling project. A family friend put up inexpensive fake-wood paneling, laid down a thin blue-green carpet without padding, and installed a suspended ceiling of Styrofoam panels. It wasn't legally a bedroom because it lacked egress windows. But it became Peggy's room, which meant we could rent one of our upstairs bedrooms to college students. It also meant that Peggy had a large room with two single beds and her own desk. The two best features of her new space were that (1) you could cause her ceiling to float up in the air if you swung the door quickly enough and (2) our house's only shower was just outside her door.

By the time Peggy started high school, our older siblings lived miles away, but our family had developed a long history with St. Cloud Tech. Five Brendens graduated from Tech over the course of two decades; Jerry even taught there for a year. Opened in 1917, the school's original location was near downtown along Lake George. The swampland there was attractive because it would provide ample space for athletics.[39] The school board apparently chose the name Technical High School in part to save a few bucks: the original name was Junior-Senior Technical High School, but the board decided that was unnecessarily long, and it could save fifty dollars in bronze lettering by shortening it. The building included a print shop where the student newspaper was published, rooms for mechanical drawing and applied arts, a commercial department with an accounting room and a typewriting room, and a large agricultural department where students learned about seed germination and animal husbandry.[40] When my family attended Tech, it offered some technical classes but also emphasized traditional academics. It was no more "technical" than any other high school in the 1970s.

St. Cloud's roots are very Catholic, so there was also a Catholic school nearby, Cathedral High School. Many of my Catholic friends and neighbors attended Cathedral, but the Brendens, as a Scandinavian Lutheran family, did not consider that an option.

Living in a conservative Midwest community like St. Cloud, Peggy wasn't exactly surrounded by feminists calling for gender equity. Many people's ideas about gender roles were as firm as the granite walls surrounding St. Cloud's Gray Stone College, the nickname for the state reformatory in town. Peggy did not have peers ready to march, demanding sports for girls. Who wanted to be labeled a fanatic, a women's libber? Just wearing pants was reason for girls to be criticized.

It never even occurred to Peggy when she started high school that she would ever play on a school tennis team. "I couldn't even imagine that there was a place where I could play on a team like the boys," she recalled. Her girlfriends weren't interested in sports. Why should they be? There weren't any teams for them. And their attempts at participating were usually met with either disapproval or mockery. Her quest to play on a tennis team would be a solitary pursuit, but Peggy still decided she wanted to make the pitch.

The letter wasn't hard to write. She knew the problem well enough to state her own case. She saw the coaching, court time, matches, and travel opportunities the boys at her school were given. There wasn't anything close for girls in any sport. Peggy did her homework and found the name of someone with the MCLU in St. Cloud, and she looked up the rule that prevented her from playing. When she finally finished typing the letter, she had explained herself plainly and with urgency:

Dear Mrs. Hartz:

Because of your interest in equal rights, I am writing to you for assistance. I am concerned with the Minnesota High School League rule which bars girls from participating [in] the boys' sports. The specific rule from the forty-ninth annual Official Handbook of the Minnesota State High School League for 1971–1972 states in Article 1, Section 8—Limitations in the Competitive Program for Boys—"Girls shall be prohibited from participation in the boys' interscholastic athletic program either as a member of the boys' team or a member of the girls' team playing the boys' team. The girls' teams shall not accept male members."

As an avid tennis player, I have played in summer tennis tournaments for several years. On the basis of the Northwestern Lawn Tennis Association 1970 rankings, I was ranked third in girls' 18 and under division. This past winter I was one of four girls selected from Minnesota to participate in the winter program, Junior Tennis Champions Inc. This summer I was a finalist in four Northwestern Lawn Tennis Association sponsored tournaments.

The high school system and local community do not provide an opportunity for an advanced girl player. Last year I was occasionally allowed to practice with the boys' team but felt like a second-class citizen since I was never allowed to compete interscholastically and my practice time was sporadic. Since I have unofficially played team members of my high school, St. Cloud Tech, I feel I could rank among the top three or four players.

I am interested in playing tennis but the girls' athletic program does not have adequate competition. Such cases as Kathryn Striebel, the St. Paul swimmer, are not unique. There are qualified girls throughout the state who, because of their sex, have not had the same opportunity to excel in sports as the boys have had. It is my firm belief that teams should be formed on the basis of ability, not sex.

Therefore, I am asking you as a member of Civil Liberties Union to initiate an effort to legally change the Minnesota State High School ruling.

Thank you for your time and consideration.

> Very truly yours,
> Peggy Brenden

P.S. Please hurry. I'm a senior.

2

KILL 'EM WITH COOL

Peggy dropped her letter in the mail in the fall of 1971, not aware of how it might affect the course of her senior year. And for most of the school year, nothing really changed. She kept walking the seven blocks to and from Tech each day. She watched television reruns of *The Mod Squad* after school, and of course, we both loved our Saturday night favorite, *The Mary Tyler Moore Show,* which spoke volumes about how a smart and funny Minnesota woman navigated independently in a man's world. (Even though I now know that Mary Tyler Moore was not from Minnesota, I'm sticking by my twelve-year-old view of the show.)

Much to our mother's dismay, the two of us kept fighting almost nightly about whose turn it was to wash the dishes. Usually, though, we operated in cahoots when it came to chores. If Mom told us to dust and vacuum, we would switch on the TV in the living room. Our mom hated this because it meant that we would sit, glazed, watching a show and never finish the assigned task. To avoid hearing a lecture about our laziness and lack of focus, Peggy devised an alert system. She would serve as lookout and hum "Yankee Doodle" as a signal for me to run to the television, quickly flip it off, and jump into dusting mode.

Lest you think Peggy was one-dimensional and only cared about sports, getting out of chores, and TV, let me add a little more about her interests. She took piano lessons for about eight years, rising before school at 5 or 6 a.m. to practice for an hour each day. I usually took the second practice shift until I quit piano lessons in junior high. Our mother somehow convinced us that one hour was the required daily minimum practice time, and we complied. Peggy was a very good pianist. She also worked as a hostess at the local Perkins restaurant. Her senior year, she took a math class at St. Cloud State College. It seemed to me she spent most weekday evenings studying in her basement bedroom. Academically, she ranked among the top ten students at Tech.

You may not find that a fascinating mix of interests and talents. But if you met Peggy, you, too, would be drawn in by her goofy stories and easy laughter. She added humor and panache to all sorts of things, whether it was the Dairy Queen chant we used on road trips or a Christmas rap for our family's holiday celebration. When our nieces or nephews came to visit, Peggy and I would cook up rhyming clues for a scavenger hunt, and the final prize would be a "lollapalooza" (better known as Kool-Aid). With one fantastical tale, told mostly straight-faced but punctuated with laughter, she nearly had me convinced I was born a chimpanzee.

Of course, a truly complete description of Peggy must include her athletic gifts. She was drawn to sports, and she was good. I know this because she always beat me in tetherball. In grade school, she was picked early for kickball. She usually scored touchdowns when we played our family Thanksgiving football games. She swam one winter on the city swim team, and she even liked climbing the huge ropes that hung from the rafters of the gymnasium. I grew up watching Peggy play whiffle ball in the backyard, and I could see she was as good as anyone in the game. In a neighborhood heavily populated by boys, Peggy played pick-up basketball in a friend's driveway, baseball at the elementary school field a few blocks away, and football at the city park just across the street. It didn't bother her that there weren't girls in the games. "I had decent skills," she explained simply. "I could throw and I could catch. Playing with those boys helped me develop those skills."

Peggy loved to compete and constantly created little games for the two of us. How many times in a row could we catch a football that was bounding down the stairs? Who could finish their chores the fastest? She infuriated me with endless rounds of "Gotcha Last," initiated with a quick poke. The game was part martial arts and part track-and-field event as we vied endlessly to get in one last shot. We arm-wrestled, thumb-wrestled, leg-wrestled, and wrestle-wrestled. Peggy frequently gave me a head start or some other small advantage to level the playing field and keep a game interesting. She adjusted the rules or padded my score so I might feel I had a fighting chance against someone more than five years older. Peggy just loved a good game.

Unfortunately, in 1971 there weren't many athletic games high school girls could play. St. Cloud Tech, with an attendance of 955 boys and 815 girls, offered only a smattering of opportunities for girls. The Girls Athletic Association provided only a few recreational activities (such as badminton, bowling, and basketball) and sponsored mini teams (gymnastics and volleyball) with very brief schedules that involved three or four competitive events per season. There were no girls' interscholastic teams with full seasons of practice, competition, uniforms, and coaching. The national participation figures reflected a similar disparity in opportunities: in the 1970–71 school year, nearly 3.5 million boys played on their high school teams compared to only 268,591 girls.[1]

For Peggy, those numbers didn't add up. Tech had no girls' tennis team—no opportunity to compete at the game in which she excelled. Peggy loved tennis. She loved the action, the skills, the competition. She loved the feeling of satisfaction that came with a hot afternoon of practice, and she thrived on the way the sport rewarded her persistence and determination. She reveled in what she called astonishing moments: "moments where my mind and body were in perfect sync, when a shot would go exactly where I aimed it, or when I'd get to a shot that should have been a lost cause. I loved those moments."

Peggy engineered her own development in a sport that was booming across the country. Tennis, like golf, had previously been tied to exclusive private clubs, the domain of wealthy men, their wives, and their children. But Peggy wasn't groomed to play tennis that way. She developed her game at the public courts that were springing up throughout Minnesota at the time. We lived within 2 miles of dozens of tennis courts built by the school district, the college, and the city of St. Cloud. Court time was free, and our parents viewed tennis as a cheap, healthy pastime. They did not invest in coaches, equipment, or special camps. Peggy wore deck shoes and white shorts for tournaments and was only marginally interested in the tennis dresses and skirts our mother sewed for her. She used a warped wooden racquet for her first tournament, having figured out how to strike the ball cleanly despite the bend in its frame.

Mom and Dad were proud of Peggy's talents, and they would go to watch some of her matches. But mostly, they stayed out of her way. Tennis was Peggy's game, and she set her own goals. "I considered them to be the perfect tennis parents because they were supportive without being oppressive," she explained. "They didn't have opinions about practice and performance and schedules and that sort of thing. Tennis was really my thing."

It was our sister Sandy and her then boyfriend, Jim Tool, who introduced Peggy to the sport when she was about ten years old. Jim was a large, barrel-chested man who loved to pound his serves and zing his forehands with plenty of topspin. Sandy stroked the ball more lightly. They were both tennis zealots. While Peggy was visiting them in Oregon, where they were working on their master's degrees, Sandy registered her for a Willamette Valley tennis tournament. The event inspired a passion for the game, thanks to a strong finish and a small trophy.[2] Peggy took group tennis lessons offered at the public parks in St. Cloud taught by Mac and Harriet Doane, who served as the city's tennis ambassadors, teaching hundreds of kids the basics of the game and later competing with them in the local tournament. By age sixteen, Peggy claimed the city's women's singles title, ending Harriet Doane's forty-year reign as St. Cloud's women's champion.

"Peggy always had good strokes, right from the beginning," Jim said. "Once she learned to play the net, she was awfully tough to beat." She developed those skills with a summer practice schedule all her own. Almost every day, she biked to the high school tennis courts about a half mile away. The five cement courts were sandwiched between the high school football stadium on one side and an alley on the other, surrounded by the city's trademark gray granite walls and topped with a chain-link fence. One of the courts was known as "the pit" because it was at a lower level, below the other courts. It had large cement walls and felt like a grassless cavern. Peggy often took the stairs down to the pit and hit ball after ball against the back wall until she improved her record of consecutive forehands or backhands. Then she would set a new goal and start again. The *kethunk* of each ball echoed in that cave and rang down the alley next to it. When the afternoon sun warmed up the pit, Peggy would cool down in the shade of a large cement culvert in one corner. She collected dozens of used balls that she kept in a laundry bag for practice, serving from one side of the court to the other, aiming for corners and lines, developing control and patience as she picked them up over and over and over.

When other people arrived at the court, Peggy sometimes snagged a pick-up partner. The regular St. Cloud tennis players recognized her, and most hit with her at some point because she was always hanging around the courts. She wasn't timid about asking people to play. She didn't hesitate to hit with old men, college students, or anyone else who just needed a brief warm-up before a partner arrived. Her regular opponents were Sandy and Jim, who, after discovering the game in college, grabbed any opportunity to play. Though they lived in another city, they visited regularly and always spent time with Peggy on the tennis court, usually as soon as they arrived.

"Sandy, Jim, and I use to spend hours hitting rock hard Tretorn tennis balls as Jim pulled them out of his carpenter's apron at the old Tech high tennis courts," Peggy wrote in her scrapbook. "Sandy and Jim also gave me my first new tennis racquet"—a wooden Dunlop Maxply "with real gut strings!"

I became Peggy's ball machine, throwing a steady stream of practice shots to one corner of the court or the other. I stood at the net armed with the laundry bag of old balls as Peggy scissor-stepped to the corners of the court and stroked down-the-line forehands or backhands. We only used white tennis balls—optic yellow balls were introduced in 1972—though many of them looked rather gray; Peggy's budget for tennis balls was limited, so the same balls remained in play for a long time. Worn and rubbed raw by the cement, a few were culled when they became lifeless and dead. Until then, I tried to throw the sad ones hard enough to get them to bounce, but it was really up to Peggy to adapt. Each ball had a different trajectory. My job was to throw them in the same place. I had spent many summer afternoons playing catch with a neighbor who lived across the street and thought I had a pretty good arm. I counted my throws, collecting a penny a toss for my work. Maybe I was a little mercenary, but I still take some credit for the strength of her down-the-line shots.

Steadily, Peggy built her game so she could put it to the test at tournaments. She scheduled her summer around a collection of competitions sponsored by the United States Tennis Association. Sometimes our parents drove her to the tournaments in Brainerd, Rochester, or even Sioux Falls. More often, the Tools accompanied her. Peggy carefully planned her calendar to include enough tournaments to earn ranking points. As a result, she accumulated boxes and boxes of trophies that she stashed behind a curtain in her basement closet. There were no trophy shelves in our living room, no engraved silver- or gold-plated statues on display. Mom didn't believe in "tooting your own horn."

Peggy's success on the courts went under the radar for the most part. Unless you played in the same tournaments she entered, you wouldn't have known how often she was winning. But her strategy and effort paid off: when the 1971 Northwestern Tennis Association rankings came out, Peggy had moved from third in the previous year to first among girls eighteen years old and under in Minnesota.

Her style of play was built on consistency. She had a smooth, fluid forehand and a strong one-handed backhand. She covered the court well, and her steady ground strokes helped her come to the net, where she finished points with well-placed volleys. The serve and volley game was somewhat unusual for women's tennis—baseline play was more the norm.

Peggy's court temperament was also quite consistent. The descendant of stoic Norwegians, she did not throw her racquet or even swear under her breath. Nor did she argue with opponents about line calls or curse or shout about her own play. In fact, she often looked so cool and unflappable that her opposition felt like she wasn't exerting herself. She perspired so lightly that sometimes she would play entire matches in her warm-up. Not given to psychological games, Peggy simply exasperated her opponents with her calm and a steely will to win. "Peggy was never nervous," Jim said.

Or, at least, not that anyone could tell.

"My attitude has always been 'Kill 'em with cool,'" Peggy explained. "I don't ever want to let my opponent know what I'm experiencing in terms of internal turmoil. My default is a Chris Evert approach: Head up. Work yourself out of this. Don't let them know when you're struggling."

Tennis legend Chris Evert, nearly the same age as Peggy, began claiming success as a professional tennis player in her teens. Known as the "Ice Maiden" because of her stone-faced and determined demeanor on the court, Evert sat atop women's tennis for nearly two decades, ranking No. 1 in the world in 1975, 1976, 1977, 1980, and 1981. Not surprisingly, she was one of Peggy's role models.

Off the court, Peggy used a similar attitude as she approached the challenge of getting on the St. Cloud Tech team. She didn't act worried, rant to friends, or yell at coaches. Our parents didn't make angry calls or write letters to the editor, either. In fact, our family hardly discussed the matter. We just waited and went on with life.

3

COURT STRATEGY

The St. Cloud Committee of the Minnesota Civil Liberties Union (MCLU) shared Peggy's plea with the MCLU staff attorney, R. Michael Wetherbee. He distributed the case report to the organization's board on November 20, 1971, and the board voted to take Peggy's case, recommending that the Minnesota High School League "abide by the U.S. Constitution in their regulations and change those regulations now in effect which are in violation of the Constitution and the Bill of Rights. If they do not comply, suit should be brought against the Minnesota State High School League for discrimination on the basis of sex in the case of Miss Peggy Brenden."[1]

Then the matter landed in the lap of Thomas Wexler, a young lawyer from the law firm Helgesen, Peterson, Engberg & Spector. A 1966 graduate of the University of Minnesota Law School, Wexler served in the army until late 1968. He was not a well-seasoned trial attorney, and he acknowledged that one of the reasons he volunteered his services with the MCLU was to expand his legal experience. Peggy's case was the first time Wexler would appear in federal court and only the fourth complete case of his career. Initially, Peggy was the only plaintiff.

The resources of the MCLU, which was staffed largely by volunteers, were being stretched increasingly thin. Each month, the board's agenda included multiple requests seeking the organization's representation, including students, teachers, police officers, and protesters. The MCLU was being overwhelmed with a continuous stream of new issues, and it simply lacked the staff, money, and volunteer attorneys to manage the volume of cases.[2] The organization hired R. Michael

Wetherbee as full-time legal counsel in 1972. Wetherbee was the first openly gay attorney employed by any ACLU affiliate. Though the national organization wasn't entirely on board, the MCLU was breaking new ground by making a concerted commitment to defending gay rights, litigating the first case in the country to argue that two men should have a right to marry.[3]

By late February 1972, the MCLU board decided to expand Peggy's case. Marie St. Pierre, mother of Antoinette (Toni) St. Pierre, had pressed the MCLU for help because Hopkins Eisenhower school administrators told her that her daughter, a cross-country runner and skier, could not participate in high school meets sponsored by the Minnesota State High School League because of her gender. The MCLU's confidential case report read, "Discrimination on the basis of sex by a public institution is in violation of the 14th Amendment and is there[fore] a civil liberties issue. It is recommended that the MCLU join this case with that of Peggy Brenden v. Minnesota State High School League (C-8971) and request the Minnesota High School League, school district 274, and Peggy Brenden's school district to abide by the U.S. Constitution in their regulations and change these regulations now in effect which are in violation of the Constitution and the Bill of Rights. If they do not comply, the MCLU should approach the State Board of Education and ask them to force compliance with the law. If the Board fails to do so, suit should be brought to stop the State Board of Education from distributing public funds to these schools."[4] The part about the State Board of Education fell away as it became apparent that the "rule" in question was set by the Minnesota State High School League, a quasi-public agency.

Though wed by common litigation, Peggy and Toni did not know each other. The MCLU combined their cases to add weight and breadth to the suit, but no one thought about personally connecting the two girls. Though each would have probably benefited from the support of a peer who understood what it felt like to take such a bold and lonely position, the girls were never introduced and knew very little about each other. My parents were cautious about spending money on long-distance phone calls. Neither family considered making the 70-mile drive to meet one another. The two girls named in the case had no sense of their alliance. They lived in two different worlds.

Still, they had similarities. They both wore glasses and often pulled their shoulder-length hair back into pigtails. They both were committed to training hard and finding ways to improve their performance. They both were well liked by the boys on their respective teams and were comfortable practicing and working out with them. Both came from schools whose teams were among the best in Minnesota. Both had a passion for their sports and loved the challenge of competition. Most importantly, Peggy and Toni both were hungry for athletic opportunities, even if others found it silly, or unfeminine, or objectionable. They were experiencing firsthand how the personal is political. "For too long, women have taken a back seat to men in athletics," Peggy said in a 1972 *St. Cloud Daily Times* story. "From grade school on up, girls simply haven't had the chance to develop their athletic skills."[5]

Despite their similarities and common plea, the two girls were also quite different. Peggy was the fourth in a family of five children. She was an academic achiever with parents who had never graduated from college. Toni was the oldest in a multigenerational household. Her mother was a school nurse with a full-time career, divorced and living with her parents. Peggy grew up in St. Cloud, an outstate Minnesota city; Toni was a recent transplant in a metro-area school district. Toni was popular and served on a social activity board to coordinate school functions. Peggy was in National Honor Society and usually skipped school parties. Toni could be fierce and fiery, letting expletives fly. Peggy prided herself on self-control, carefully holding her emotions in check. None of those things mattered when the court case started. They were simply sorted into one classification: "girls."

Wexler knew very little about Peggy and Toni personally and did not become acquainted with the two high schoolers. He contacted the principals at both high schools as well as the Minnesota State High School League to see whether it was possible to resolve the matter without litigation. That didn't work. So he focused on the facts and the law. He had his hands full. "By the time the case got to me, the athletic season for their respective sports was fast upon us," Wexler recalled. "I didn't want to make it a class action. It would have taken more time, and I had a nice, clean case. I had noncontact sports. And I didn't have to deal with why girls should be allowed to wrestle or play football. That introduced new elements that would have made the case more complicated and possibly jeopardize the chance of winning it. I had a nice, simple, clean case with a tennis player and a cross-country runner, and I just wanted to keep it that way. I didn't want to add more parties."

In a typical class-action suit, a plaintiff sues a defendant on behalf of a group, or class. It is usually used when a large number of people have been harmed by the same defendant or defendants in a similar way, such as in *Brown v. Board of Education,* in which Oliver Brown and a group of fellow parents in Topeka, Kansas, challenged their school system's racial segregation. According to ACLU records from the 1970s, the organization did not encourage class actions, pointing to the courts' role in approving settlements and the way an unfavorable settlement could hurt the success of other suits.[6]

Rather than recruiting girls from all over the state who might want to play on a boys' sports team, Wexler felt that focusing on Peggy and Toni would offer a greater chance of success and accomplish the same goal. He believed that winning this case would create a chink in the armor of the high school athletic system built with boys in mind. It would provide the impetus necessary to push high schools, and the Minnesota High School League, to develop athletic opportunities for girls so they wouldn't be confronted with similar challenges. The MSHSL's rule banning girls from competing with boys blocked Peggy and Toni, who attended schools without a girls' team, from equal access. Wexler's strategy was straightforward: build the case as a violation of the Fourteenth Amendment and civil rights statute. Forbidding these two girls, who were capable of competing effectively, from playing on their schools' sports teams was arbitrary and unreasonable. If no alternative was provided, they were not being given equal protection as required by the Fourteenth Amendment.

It was Toni's mother who made the plea to persuade the MCLU to take her daughter's case. My parents did not play that same role.

Still, our father, Torbin Brenden (known as Toby), was a named plaintiff largely because Peggy was a minor and the courts required that an adult be named on her behalf. (It is not clear why my mother, Esther Brenden, wasn't also named.) Dad's role was mostly confined to driving to the courthouse and providing brief testimony. Reporters didn't ask to interview him—it was Peggy's name in the news. The brief letter she had sent in October triggered media glare on April 5, 1972, when the case was filed in United States District Court for the District of Minnesota.

The unexpected notoriety made Peggy uncomfortable. It was startling to see her full name in banner headlines as she arrived home from school. She recalled, "I remember picking up the *St. Cloud Daily Times* laying on our front step, and on the top it said, 'Peggy Brenden Sues School District.' I thought, 'Oh my gosh, this is much bigger than I ever imagined.' That's the first moment I knew that this was going to be something other people would talk about." For a teenager who preferred to blend in, the media coverage did not feel like a moment in the sun—it was just plain disconcerting. Upon leaving school one day, Peggy was accosted by a reporter who shoved a microphone into her face. "I remember being very self-conscious about it, wanting to do my best to be articulate and feeling like I was just an idiot," she said.

Newspapers all over the state announced the filing of a lawsuit by two teenage girls against the MSHSL and their respective school districts. The St. Cloud headlines read, "Peggy Brenden Sues St. Cloud District to Play High School Sports" and "Tech Senior Might Set Precedent, Wants Spot on Varsity Tennis Team." The Hopkins newspaper seemed to assume Toni was a recognized name and used the headline "Toni, Lawsuit Seek 'Good Competition.'" Minneapolis and St. Paul were less personal in their approach: "2 Girls Sue State Prep League" and "Suit Filed to Place Girls on Boys' Athletic Teams."[7]

Initially, it appeared the St. Cloud School District (District 742) might actually stand with Peggy in her suit against the MSHSL. At least one article suggested it might "fight the rule and back the girl."[8] Days later, in an article headlined "District 742 against Girl on Boys' Team," St. Cloud school administrators claimed the district was "neutral" on Peggy's request to play on the boys' team. Yet the district hired its own attorney to oppose Peggy and the MCLU. Superintendent Kermit Eastman said the real issue was "far broader than whether or not Technical High School should allow a girl on its boys interscholastic tennis team."

"The issue is whether or not the rule should be permitted to stand that prohibits a girl from participating on any boys interscholastic team," Eastman said, adding that the school district was also concerned "reverse discrimination" could result. And there were other ramifications to consider, such as what sort of supervision, physical care, coaching, or injuries might result from mixed-gender sports.[9] The school district chose to use the courtroom to sort out those issues and fight Peggy's request to play tennis.

So, as is often the case in litigation, the "real issue" became many things: whether the court should be able to overturn an MSHSL rule, whether allowing these girls to play against boys would undermine the future development of all girls' athletic opportunities, whether mixing girls and boys on sports teams would create dire problems and risks for students and their schools. Throughout the hearing, the four attorneys and the judge would find themselves continually trying to define the "real issue."

Brenden v. Independent School District 742 started out as just another case for Wexler, but he soon saw there were many people interested in the outcome. He was fielding calls from people who wanted to weigh in on his strategy. Working solo, he didn't feel as though he had time to consult or reconfigure his plans. He stopped taking the phone calls.

Wexler was facing the task of carving new constitutional dimensions amid a cast of big Minnesota names, prominent among them the federal judge assigned to the matter: Honorable Miles W. Lord. A friend of Vice President Hubert Humphrey and Minnesota senators Walter Mondale and Eugene McCarthy, Lord, in 1966 at the age of forty-six, was nominated for a federal judgeship by President Lyndon Johnson. Humphrey called Lord "the people's judge." He was known for a Wild West approach to his work. Mondale described him as "a different kind of public servant because he listened to his own drummer." The judge loved the media limelight and sought it out. In fact, he happily relied upon at least one law clerk, Roberta Walburn, a former newspaper reporter and later biographer, to be a "de facto press agent."[10]

One of Lord's biggest cases (*United States v. Reserve Mining Co.*, in which the Justice Department accused Reserve Mining Company, one of Minnesota's largest employers, of violating federal pollution laws) launched at nearly the same time as Peggy and Toni's court challenge. In April 1972, Lord presided over a preliminary hearing in that legal battle, which would dominate the headlines for years.[11] He eventually halted the dumping of taconite tailings in Lake Superior by Reserve Mining, issuing an injunction that completely shut down the company's operations and "essentially put more than three thousand workers out on the street without a job."[12] In the injunction, Lord accused the company of "economic blackmail," using the company's employees as "hostages" so that the court would permit the "continued exposure of known human carcinogens to the cities of Duluth and other North Shore Communities."[13]

Born on northern Minnesota's Iron Range, Lord felt strongly about the deadly health hazards associated with the tailings that mining companies dumped into the Lake Superior basin, the source of much of the region's drinking water. "The defendants are daily endangering the lives of thousands of people," Lord wrote in his May 1974 injunction. "This court cannot honor profit over human life and, therefore, has no other choice but to abate the discharge."[14] The U.S. Court of Appeals later removed Lord from the Reserve Mining case, stating, "Judge Lord seems to have shed the robe of the judge and assumed the mantle of the advocate."[15]

"I tried to put the spotlight on the big boys, the rich, the overprivileged," he would later say of his tactics.[16] "I think the educational function [of the bench] is very important. And I also think that publicizing what you say is important. It isn't so important to have something in the law books because nobody reads the law books, except other lawyers. It's important to give vent publicly to what it is you're deciding and why you are deciding it."

Whatever Judge Lord decided in Peggy's case, he would not do it quietly. Even as a teenager, Peggy could see he was hardly a reserved and quiet courtroom presence. "He was not shy about inserting himself into the proceedings," she said looking back.

Asked many years later about the assignment of Lord to the case, Wexler smiled and said simply, "That was fortunate. Whatever deficiencies I may have exhibited in the trial process as a young lawyer, he certainly filled in and did a lot of the work." Lord suggested to him early on that he might need some assistance for such a substantial and complicated case. But Wexler moved on single-handedly—not out of ego but out of efficiency. "I knew it was a high-profile case," he said. "And I felt the pressure of handling that kind of case. Some people were calling me and wanting to have some input on how I did it, and I just didn't have enough time for that."

From the bench, Lord would question witnesses throughout the case. Sometimes he butted heads with attorneys. "I did considerable cross-examination of the witness[es] myself," Lord admitted. "Since there was no jury there to be prejudiced, I thought it appropriate that I could ask questions as they occurred to me. Plaintiffs' counsel did not object, but the heat emanating from the defendant's table was almost palpable."[17]

Representing the MSHSL was Bernhard W. LeVander, former chair of the Minnesota Republican Party and younger brother of Harold LeVander, who had been Minnesota's governor from 1967 to 1971. Bernhard LeVander frequently defended the league against challenges to its eligibility rules and was quite proud of a 1970 Minnesota Supreme Court decision, *Brown v. Wells,* that had made him a cause célèbre in high school league circles.[18] In that case, a boy at Roosevelt High School in Minneapolis wanted to participate in an outside hockey league *and* compete on his school's hockey team. The MSHSL said no. A district court judge sided with the Roosevelt student, but upon appeal, the Minnesota Supreme Court asserted that "courts should not be called upon to arbitrate the reasonableness of League rules unless objectors are prepared to demonstrate that they are not supported by reason or adopted in good conscience." It ruled the league's eligibility rules must be upheld "unless those regulations are clearly arbitrary and unreasonable."[19]

Lord and LeVander had political history together. LeVander had been the Republican nominee and Lord's opponent in his first campaign to become attorney general of Minnesota in 1954. At that time, Lord chose to largely ignore LeVander, instead campaigning against the incumbent governor, Republican C. Elmer Anderson. "Why donate to my opponent any free publicity?"[20] Lord explained later. In fact, Lord challenged Anderson, not LeVander, to a televised debate. The governor failed to appear, leaving Lord the opportunity to conduct a one-way debate. The results: he won the debate and the election.

LeVander felt Lord had used "shoddy tactics" in the campaign. In his memoir, he wrote, "I have never had any respect for Miles Lord." LeVander described his take on their shared 1954 attorney general campaign:

> One of the things he pulled was the old "empty-chair" trick, where he invited C. Elmer Anderson, the weakest link on our ticket, to debate him on the radio. And, of course, Elmer didn't show up and Lord used that in campaign statements, ads and so on. It was a pure and simple means of getting himself some publicity. He was very clever in getting publicity. I had solicited the support of lawyers in the state and had an ad with 800-plus lawyers supporting me. I later learned that Lord kept a copy of that ad in his desk and after he became attorney general, if any of those who had supported me asked for any help or assistance, Lord would deny them their request.[21]

Not surprisingly, the air was tense between the two men in the courtroom.

LeVander would lean heavily on the testimony of Dorothy McIntyre, assistant executive director of the MSHSL. Hired in the spring of 1970, she was the first woman selected as an executive staff member. The league used her voice to bolster its defense, and she would play a key role in articulating its position.

Lord was not fond of the MSHSL, later referring to it as the "jock strap brigade."[22] As attorney general, he had jousted with the league in 1956 when the New Prague school district asked him to rule "on the legality of the MSHSL and the legal right of high schools to join the League." The district was unhappy with an eligibility rule that prevented two high school players from participating in interscholastic competition because they had played in an independent amateur baseball "all-star" game the previous summer.[23] "I had some experience with the State High School League and it wasn't very pleasant," Lord said of the case. "I ruled that it didn't exist, that there was no legislative authority for it to exist. As a result . . . I lost my seat at the state high school basketball tournaments, and they moved me up behind a post. Yeah, I sat behind a post . . ." Within months of his ruling, a bill was passed in the 1957 legislative session granting school boards the right to join associations sponsoring interscholastic activities. And by late May 1957, Attorney General Lord ruled that the questions submitted in the original complaint were moot.

Several of Lord's family members expressed interest and concern about how he might handle a case dealing with girls' athletic opportunities. Though he was no fan of the league, Lord also sported a thick streak of chauvinism. The judge understood that referring to lawyers or staff members as "girls" was out of bounds, but still he adopted his own facetious alternatives ("woman-person" or "lawyerette") and generally liked to use diminutive terms to refer to women. In fact, upon being assigned to Peggy's case, he made a crack to his son-in-law that perhaps he would get to preside over a case for girls who wanted to wrestle with boys. He considered that a joke.

"He wasn't taking women seriously," said his daughter Priscilla, who listened to her father describe the case over the phone as she held her newborn baby, Maggie, at the hospital. She worried that he didn't appreciate the plight of these two high school girls and did not hesitate to share her opinion. "This is just not fair, that the boys get to do this, but the girls don't," she told him angrily. "Dad, I would have given anything to play hockey with the boys, or the girls. But there wasn't that opportunity."[24]

Judge Lord sought out the opinion of his older sister Rilla, who had played on a girls' basketball team in northern Minnesota in the early 1920s. He recalled her telling him, "Miles, you remember up at Crosby when we would play basketball and the girls would wear those old black bloomers and white middies? We used old wobbly basketballs. We had to *make* our own uniforms. Then, when the boys were ready to play, they came out in their nice uniforms, paid for by the school district. . . . Nice round balls for the boys. 'Girls, off the court,' came the order, and off we went. The boys took over the gym, wearing woolen sweatsuits and bouncing new basketballs paid for by the school. 'Miles, you think about it!' she said."

Priscilla's and Rilla's comments bothered Lord, forcing him to wrestle with his own attitudes about what rights and privileges ought to accompany gender. According to Priscilla, her father rarely polled family members for their thoughts on a case, but he wanted a woman's perspective. "He was, I would say, right on the precipice of seeing, understanding how women were not included," she said.

Judge Lord pushed to fast-track the case, moving very quickly, especially by federal court standards. The plaintiffs' request for preliminary and permanent injunctive relief required an evidentiary hearing before a judge, but it did not require a jury. The first day of hearings was scheduled for April 24, 1972, and Judge Lord never lost sight of the importance of a speedy trial.

Peggy felt the clock ticking. Toni had another year of high school ahead, but Peggy's plea to play on the boys' team would become a moot issue if a decision wasn't made before the tennis season ended. She saw Tech's season marching on without her. Some matches had been postponed or rescheduled, as often happens due to Minnesota's fickle spring weather, and the team's first actual match was April 17 against Little Falls. But without a court decision, Peggy couldn't be a full-fledged member of the team or play an official match.

At Peggy's request, Bill Ritchie did find her an opponent.[25] Coach Ritchie often set up exhibition matches so players outside the starting lineup could practice match play. Akin to scrimmages, these exhibition matches were more informal and were dependent upon many things: weather, travel time, court and player availability. "I let the opposing coach know that Peggy was coming, and he would get one of the girls," Ritchie said, noting that the other coaches were aware of how well Peggy played. The school's official team score was still based only on the top three singles and top two doubles matches. Even though the match was unofficial, the Little Falls coach dared not pit Peggy against any boys on his team. On that cold, cloudy day, the Tech team won 5-0 and Peggy defeated her Little Falls opponent, Margaret Witt, 6–0, 6–0.[26]

From that point on, Tech's tennis team played matches two or three times a week. "It was frustrating to see Peggy sit out match after match," Jim Tool said. "But at least the coach let her practice. Not every coach would have done that."

For Peggy, the season was fast disappearing.

Since time was so short, there were very few filings and legal maneuvers in advance of the April hearing. Wexler filed a petition for a preliminary injunction—a temporary order compelling the MSHSL to set aside its rule barring girls from boys' teams only for Peggy and Toni. If granted, it would mean Peggy could play official tennis for the rest of the spring. As a senior, her plea had immediacy and required the court to act promptly. The preliminary injunction would also give Toni a chance to compete on the boys' cross-country running and skiing teams the following school year. It didn't mention any other athletes.

In a pretrial conference between the attorneys and Judge Lord just twelve days before the scheduled hearing, Lord suggested that Peggy be allowed to play with the team without any formal court order. But LeVander said MSHSL rules made that impossible. Lord asked, "Why should the League be so brittle?"[27]

But the MSHSL was not going to budge from its position: girls could not play on boys' teams—ever, under any circumstances. "I was impressed by the vigor of the high school league's opposition to what to me seemed like a pretty reasonable and obvious accommodation that ought to be made," Wexler said. He felt that the organization's position was to "remain consistently firm and unyielding . . . It almost seemed like there was a sense on the part of high school league officials that their system would crumble if their rules weren't strictly enforced." In discussions before the hearing, the message

Wexler heard from McIntyre was "If we let the girls get on the boys' teams, then the school districts won't be motivated to create equivalent systems for the girls." McIntyre was, he said, "the driving force behind the position that the high school league took. She was the voice of women's sports; she was very capable; she was well spoken and well regarded."

McIntyre was committed to building girls' athletic opportunities and argued that this case could derail those efforts. "The public schools of Minnesota are charged with the responsibility of educating the masses," she said in a deposition. "Our school programs cannot place emphasis on the needs of the individual to the exclusion of the needs of the group." In a portion of her sworn testimony aimed specifically at Peggy, McIntyre stated that it was "educationally unsound" for Peggy to participate on a boys' team, and it would have a "devastating and disastrous effect on both girls' and boys' athletic programs." She contended that Tech already provided a tennis program that was "substantial and affords an excellent opportunity for advancing her skills." "Any benefit that possibly could come to Peggy would indeed be slight compared to the widespread doubt, uncertainty and confusion that would be created by" allowing her to play tennis with boys, she said.[28]

The complaint filed on behalf of the girls stated emphatically that the MSHSL rule deprived them of an "opportunity, like that available to male students," keeping them from elevating their standards of sportsmanship, responsible citizenship, and athletic skills. It noted that the MSHSL was "financed largely by public tax revenues and that the amount of such revenues expended on the boys' program is greater than and grossly disproportionate to the revenues expended on the girls' program."[29]

Not coincidentally, a week before the federal court hearing, the St. Cloud school board met and OK'd a girls' sports plan. Superintendent Eastman made no mention of Peggy's case and claimed the district had not been "rushed or pressured" into its decision. In fact, he said, it had been considering the matter for more than a year. But he did note, "It seems likely that court decisions could dictate greater consideration for athletic programs for girls." The school board

authorized the Tech and Apollo athletic directors to seek approval
from the MSHSL for girls' interscholastic programs, but Eastman did
not commit to a timetable for implementing a list of possible girls'
teams, stating that they would be "developed as the need arises."[30]

Meanwhile, the boys' tennis season marched on. Peggy attended
practices but still had no place in the team lineup without a court
decision. She did play another exhibition match in Litchfield, where
coach Greg Mathews knew exactly whom he would pit against Peggy:
junior Jody Nolen. Though it was an exhibition match rather than a
regulation match, Mathews would characterize it as an act of defiance. Jody had tried out for her school's tennis team her sophomore
year with Mathews's support. The coach, a social studies teacher,
said he viewed her participation on the tennis team as a civil rights
issue. Though some opposing coaches were upset at the prospect of
pitting their male players against Jody, Mathews countered that the
game wasn't about gender; they were playing another human being.
Still, for her sophomore and junior years, Jody played only exhibition matches, even as her younger brother Billy played nearly all the
team's regulation matches. "Jody has practiced for two years with our
team with no hope of ever playing," Mathews said at the time. "That's
dedication. She works harder than any boy on my squad."[31] Peggy
beat Jody Nolen 6–3, 6–2.[32] Coach Mathews would later refer to Jody
and Peggy as "the Jackie Robinsons of girls' tennis."[33]

Meanwhile, Sue Fischer, a senior at St. Cloud Cathedral High
School, encountered fewer obstacles in her athletic career. She was
able to claim the number-one singles spot on her school's newly
formed and only tennis team, which her father coached. Cathedral was
part of the Minnesota Independent High School League, composed
of parochial and private schools. That league had no rules forbidding
girls from playing against boys. "I didn't have to argue; I didn't have
to fight about it," Fischer said. "I was just eligible." There were still
awkward moments, however, when the Cathedral team would arrive
at a match and watch as other coaches and players discussed whether
they would actually field an opponent to play against a girl. Fischer
would become the first girl to earn a letter in sports at Cathedral.

All over the state, girls from both public and parochial schools were rocking the boat, asking for athletic opportunities. But they had not joined together. The MSHSL estimated that more than eighty girls wanted a chance to compete with boys.[34] Each stood as an exception, pleading for equal treatment in a system built for boys. With Peggy and Toni's case, a federal court would publicly weigh in on the issue, setting a precedent—giving girls clout when they asked to participate. Their case announced to school boards, coaches, administrators, and the high school league that girls expected the same opportunities as boys.

The two girls' classmates, coaches, and teammates would later contend they were behind them. But if so, it was largely passive support. The Tech student council president, who would go on to become a motivational speaker, lauded the efforts of Tech's student government to help Peggy's cause in a 2015 interview for a National Student Council publication. Unfortunately, Peggy was unaware of any student council support, and it was never mentioned in the student newspaper, either. With decades of hindsight, siding with a girl who wanted to play tennis on the only team available seems obvious, but in 1972 few peers voiced their support directly. Most of the support came well after the case was decided.

Peggy said she didn't feel harassed by her teammates, competitors, or coaches; no one confronted her in "a negative way." In fact, she recalls her teammates kidding about the litigation and her presence on the team, but it wasn't "mean-spirited." Perhaps that is the most overt support a high school kid in 1972 could expect. Mostly the suit was an elephant in the room; it wasn't the subject of conversations and was only barely acknowledged. The two girls had to negotiate the experience on their own. Peggy didn't think her friends were interested, and she didn't bring it up. "I just wanted to get through it," she said. Our parents admitted they fielded some "crank calls" related to the case, but they kept the contents of those conversations to themselves.

Peggy doubted the legal system could move fast enough for her purposes. "To be able to turn this around in time for me to have any chance to play was going to be something just short of a miracle," she said. "But it seemed to take on a life of its own."

Wexler, who was tackling a crash course in constitutional law, initially found little legal precedent to lean on. Fortunately, he was able to consult with another ACLU litigator who had valuable experience. Ruth Bader Ginsburg, not yet an associate justice of the Supreme Court of the United States, was serving as coordinator for the ACLU's Women's Rights Project, which was designed to challenge laws that discriminated against women in an era when gender discrimination in the law was common. Using the Fourteenth Amendment, which was originally aimed at racial discrimination, Ginsburg sought to convince the courts that gender-based discrimination was unconstitutional. She argued that it was analogous to race discrimination, both being arbitrary forms of unequal treatment.[35] She took a commonsense approach: that "people should not be treated differently for no good reason" and that the Constitution prohibited clearly irrational discrimination against women.[36]

In 1971 Ginsburg cowrote a groundbreaking brief for a case before the U.S. Supreme Court, *Reed v. Reed.* She explained:

> The case was commenced by Sally Reed of Boise, Idaho, who had a young son. She and her husband separated. When the son was, quote, "of tender years," she was the custodian, but when the boy was ready to be prepared for a man's world, the judge— the family court judge—thought the boy should live at least part of the time in his father's house. Sally was very distressed about that and for good reason. The boy became tremendously depressed and one day took out one of his father's many rifles to kill himself. Sally wanted to be appointed administrator of his estate. She applied for the appointment and then, about two weeks later, her former husband applied. The probate court judge told Sally, "The law decides this question for me. It reads, "As between persons equally entitled to administer a decedent's estate, males must be preferred to females."[37]

The Idaho Code gave strict preference to men over women to avoid costly and cumbersome hearings to determine competency. Ginsburg argued forcefully that this was unconstitutional: "To eliminate women who share an eligibility category with a man, when there is no basis in fact to assume that women are less competent to administer than are men, is patently unreasonable and constitutionally impermissible. A woman's right to equal treatment may not be sacrificed to expediency."[38]

The Supreme Court, which had never used the Fourteenth Amendment to strike down a law on the basis of gender, decided to invalidate the Idaho statute. In so doing, it extended the Constitution's equal protection guarantee to women for the first time.[39] Chief Justice Warren E. Burger wrote in his opinion, "To give a mandatory preference to members of either sex over members of the other, merely to accomplish the elimination of hearings on the merits, is to make the very kind of arbitrary legislative choice forbidden by the Equal Protection Clause of the Fourteenth Amendment; and whatever may be said as to the positive values of avoiding intrafamily controversy, the choice in this context may not lawfully be mandated solely on the basis of sex."[40]

The ACLU continued to build on that decision with targeted litigation intended to clarify women's status and constitutional rights. Ginsburg led the charge, helping attorneys like Thomas Wexler by offering her experience and sharing her work product. He was grateful for a brief she provided to bolster his research.

Ginsburg represented another high school girl in a 1972 case very similar to Wexler's. Abbe Seldin was a fifteen-year-old girl who wanted to try out for the boys' varsity tennis team at Teaneck High School. Like the MSHSL, the New Jersey State Interscholastic Association, a nongovernmental agency that supervises school sports events among its members, had a rule against mixed-gender athletic competition. Ginsburg and another ACLU attorney represented Abbe in federal district court in Newark; midway through the trial, the association decided to change the rule, giving Abbe the opportunity to play tennis with the team.[41] The case was settled by starting a one-year pilot program in which schools without a separate interscholastic girls' team could allow girls to participate on boys' teams.[42]

In the early 1970s, Americans were becoming more aware of systematic gender discrimination blocking the path of girls and women. As Wexler prepared his case for Peggy and Toni, Congress was considering a ban on gender-based discrimination in public-supported educational settings.[43] On February 28, 1972, Birch Bayh of Indiana explained to fellow senators that his amendment, which would later become known as Title IX, was "an important first step in the effort to provide for the women of America something that is rightfully theirs—an equal chance to attend the schools of their choice, to develop the skills they want, and to apply those skills with the knowledge that they will have a fair chance to secure the jobs of their choice with equal pay for equal work."[44] Bayh offered extensive evidence illustrating how the American educational system unjustifiably discriminated against women by preferring men for admissions and financial aid, offering sex-segregated vocational programs, and failing to admit, hire, or equitably pay women in graduate schools and faculty ranks. He never brought up athletics.

Many women thought participating in sports was the least of their worries. Girls and women had long been conditioned to view sports as being outside their domain, so they saw no need to fight for participation or equality. They did not see how sports mirrored the many ways society limited women and girls by restricting their opportunities. But *Sports Illustrated* proclaimed in its May 28, 1973, cover story:

> There is no sharper example of discrimination today than that which operates against girls and women who take part in competitive sports . . . The funds, facilities, coaching, rewards and honors allowed women are grossly inferior to those granted men. In many places absolutely no support is given to women's athletics, and females are barred by law, regulation, tradition or hostility of males from sharing athletic resources and pleasures.[45]

The headline: "Women are getting a raw deal."

Billie Jean King kept trying to make that point. A nationally ranked tennis player who, at age seventeen, won the women's doubles championship at Wimbledon, she was never offered an athletic scholarship.[46] King entered Los Angeles State College in 1961 and struggled with tight finances, eventually dropping out of school to make a commitment to her tennis career. As a pro, she won big tournaments, yet the media referred to her as the "bouncy girl" and a California housewife. When she was in her early twenties, reporters were already asking when she would retire because the notion that a woman might have a career in athletics was so absurd to them. Men collected prize money eight to twelve times as high as women playing in the same tournaments. Organizers contended women didn't draw as large a crowd or work as hard. King developed a women-only tournament and then a women's tour in 1971. "I wanted the chance to make money, honest money, doing what I did best," she explained.[47]

In 1971 King became the first woman athlete to win $100,000 in a year. That same year, however, Rod Laver collected $290,000 as the leader on the men's tennis circuit—and King had to win three times as many tournaments as Laver to claim just over one-third of his take-home pay.[48] When she was finally able to cash in on her popularity through endorsement earnings, King chose to improve women's athletic opportunities by financing *womenSports* magazine and founding the Women's Sports Foundation, an advocacy group that challenged sexism in sport.[49]

The sports world revolved around men. Women and girls who sought to participate were made to feel like supplicants, unworthy and inadequate. But Peggy and Toni weren't going to accept that role. They would not wait for a better deal. They had an appointment in a federal courtroom to advocate for gender equity.

4

TAKING THE STAND

On Monday, April 24, 1972, Toby, Esther, and Peggy Brenden traveled to the U.S. courthouse in Minneapolis. Our parents seldom drove to downtown Minneapolis, with its exasperating traffic, parking, and crowds. Likely they had some argument about navigation, which was always a sore point between them. Toby did not think Esther was good with maps. She hadn't gotten her driver's license until she was in her thirties or forties. Our father, unquestionably, was the driver in our family, a traveling salesman accustomed to spending most of his day in the car—largely in rural Minnesota communities like Brooten, Belgrade, and Montevideo, or small towns in South Dakota. He rarely drove through large cities. The three of them would have left early, very early, hoping to avoid heavy morning traffic. Our mother probably perked a thermos of coffee using the grounds left over from the previous day. She typically packed homemade sandwiches and chocolate-chip cookies for the road.

No one in my family had ever set foot in a federal courthouse before. The Brendens weren't the sort of people to "make a federal case" out of anything. We were raised to neither whine nor complain. Lawsuits and attorneys were foreign to us.

Though I did not have a front-row seat in the courtroom, I have something better: a typewritten transcript of the proceedings, three volumes and more than five hundred pages covering, verbatim, what was stated for the record. The language seems strange, formal, and awkward at times, and there aren't any notes about the tone of voice, facial expressions, or body language of the speakers. Still, the transcript gives a blow-by-blow narrative of the attorneys' arguments, the witnesses' testimony, and the judge's rulings and comments.[1]

This case had landed in a federal courthouse because of its constitutional subject matter. The complaint stated that public tax dollars were being spent disproportionately on high school boys' athletics compared to girls' and that the Minnesota State High School League rule barring girls from athletic teams was unconstitutional because it denied equal protection as required by the Fourteenth Amendment. As a civil action arising under the U.S. Constitution, the case belonged in federal court, not state court. At the time, the federal courts also had a minimum "amount in controversy" requirement of $10,000, so that is precisely the amount Wexler set. Within the first ten minutes of the course proceedings, however, he offered to drop the demand for monetary damages—that was not the motivation for the case. Minnesota State High School League attorney Bernhard LeVander wanted more than damages to be dropped: he wasted no time in asking that the entire case be dropped. As soon as the "good mornings" were finished, he began arguing for a dismissal.

"Could I hold you up, please," Judge Lord said. He was not about to allow LeVander to derail the hearing before it even started. "To properly consider and adjudicate the problem of whether or not the case should be dismissed would take considerable time." He went on to state that he often ruled against the party seeking a dismissal and that resolving the case with a decision would be far more satisfactory. "What I would like to do, Mr. LeVander, is to take it on your brief and deny it and move onto the merits."

The attorney for the Hopkins School District, J. Dennis O'Brien, then raised his own concerns. His client hadn't given him direction about where it stood—the school board had not actually decided its position and intended to meet the following evening to determine its stance. "In all candor, I should point out to the Court, for the Court's assistance, that I have a divided board on this question. I am not sure how the issue will be resolved," O'Brien said. "There are some members of the school board that would like to join in the plaintiffs' action and there are some members that would oppose that action. So at this point I would like to state that the defendant, Hopkins School Board, has not taken a formal position on the rules here in question."

"Very well," Judge Lord replied. "What about St. Cloud?"

Michael Donohue, the attorney representing St. Cloud's Independent School District (ISD) 742, said his client intended to uphold the rule forbidding girls from boys' teams because it saw "too many ramifications with girls on boys' teams or boys on girls' teams."

Then Judge Lord emphasized the court's interest in moving efficiently, directing this point to LeVander in particular. Lord knew the MSHSL attorney had a long list of witnesses lined up, many of them experts in physiology and physical education who would testify about the rationale and educational validity for the rule. The judge noted that there might be ways to streamline that testimony, although he made no particular rulings or demands. In the end, seventeen people testified from Monday through Wednesday.

Wexler started by focusing on Peggy's and Toni's desire and ability to compete effectively with the boys. "Our case was to put the coaches and girls on the stand," he explained. Neither he nor Peggy remembers meeting the other before appearing at the courthouse. Peggy thinks she may have had a phone conversation to help her prepare to testify. "I was a small part of the evidence," she said. After Wexler was assigned to her case, she wrote him a letter with a few details about her interactions with the coach and thanked him for representing her.

In the courtroom, Wexler opened by stating the narrow limits of his request. "We are asking that these girls, because there are no girls' teams at their schools, be allowed to try to qualify for those boys' teams," he said. "Of course, it's hard to ignore that the larger proposition, as established, is going to be that all the girls that find themselves in similar situations should be allowed to do likewise. But for the purposes of our action here today, we do not have a class action."

Judge Lord responded, "You do not have a class action?"

Wexler answered, "We do not."

Judge Lord said, "Absent a class action, I would think that my ruling would be basically confined to the two persons involved here."

Lord would return to this point repeatedly during testimony. As witnesses attempted to generalize about the performance and problems associated with adding girls to high school sports teams, he would press them to narrow their focus to just the two girls named in the lawsuit: Peggy and Toni.

Peggy was the first person to testify. The transcript does not betray a tremor in her voice or tension in her face. I think she used the same approach in the courtroom as the tennis court: kill 'em with cool. She stepped to the front of the courtroom and took the oath. She spelled her name; gave her birthdate, her address, and her relationship to Torbin Brenden; and identified herself as a senior at Tech who was to graduate in June. Then Wexler asked her why she wanted to play tennis at St. Cloud Technical High School. "I guess the biggest reason is because I enjoy the competition," she answered. "It's a personal challenge, as well as a chance to improve my game and skills." Peggy testified that she had participated in the school's "extramural" girls' tennis program, held the previous fall. The organizers had originally planned for it to include four one-hour sessions of play; unfortunately, bad weather drastically cut into the girls' court time. The participants were supervised, but not coached, and they practiced with one another rather than competing against other schools.

On cross-examination, the MSHSL attorney asked Peggy more about her tennis experience, emphasizing the many opportunities she had to develop her game. As far as I can tell, it was a classic catch-22. On the one hand, LeVander was calling experts to testify that girls could not successfully compete with boys. On the other hand, he painted Toni and Peggy as "exceptional" girls with ample opportunities to use their skills who were demanding special treatment. He asked about Peggy's private lessons and coaches. She explained that she had no coach and her instruction had been in the community's summer recreation program.

Judge Lord asked, "How is this relevant?"

LeVander replied, "I think it's relevant for the purpose of showing, Your Honor, that this girl has had very unusual and exceptional experience and public schools shouldn't be obligated to serve students in her particular 'situation.'"

Wexler responded that while he would agree Peggy had "significant tennis activity outside the school," he wondered whether the same could be said of the boys on the team. The St. Cloud School District attorney said he didn't know and would need to find out.

LeVander asked Peggy whether there were any other girls who wanted to be on the boys' tennis team. "To my knowledge, there aren't," she answered. He then asked how she would rank on the team. This type of question would come up throughout the hearing—even though Peggy and Toni were asking to play on teams that made no cuts and welcomed any boy who wished to participate, regardless of skill, several witnesses were asked to rate or compare the girls' athletic skills to boys'. Peggy estimated that she would rank fourth or fifth on the varsity roster of seven players.

Our father was called to testify next. Besides asking how many years he had resided in the St. Cloud School District and whether he paid real estate taxes in the state of Minnesota, Wexler asked him whether he wanted to see Peggy play on the tennis team and whether he encouraged her. The answer to both questions: "Yes, I do."

When it was the MSHSL's turn, LeVander asked him whether he would be satisfied if Tech had a girls' interscholastic sports program for Peggy. My dad seldom disagreed with anyone, but he knew this was a hypothetical question that would not serve his daughter well. "Well, of course, the time has passed now where [the school district] could get such a program going," he said. "So that couldn't possibly satisfy her wishes now."

LeVander persisted, asking whether our dad, "as a parent, looked into the question of whether physically and physiologically, it would be a happy thing" for Peggy to "tax herself by competing with a boy in boys' competition."

That was not a concern, our father replied: "I think that she is very able, physically, and she certainly has gone through the rigors of conditioning . . . I feel she wouldn't be trying to do this unless she felt she was capable of doing it."

LeVander's "happy thing" question was one of many that he would pose about the effect mixed-gender competition would have on athletes. The MSHSL trotted out an extensive array of experts to testify about the problems associated with girls competing against boys. LeVander also pressed our father to outline his efforts to talk to the school board, school officials such as the principal or superintendent, or league authorities to resolve the issue. He said he had not contacted anyone about the issue. Wexler noted that four to six weeks before the lawsuit commenced, he had contacted the principals of both girls' high schools on their behalf and was told the schools were bound by the league rule and there was nothing they could do about it. He had also contacted Dorothy McIntyre of the MSHSL about the problem and found little hope in pushing the league to administratively make changes to allow the girls to play.

LeVander said he did not think what Wexler described "constituted an exhaustion of administrative remedies." Michael Donohue chimed in that St. Cloud Tech's principal had been contacted "just this March" about the matter and the school board had authorized a plan to add interscholastic tennis for girls in the future. LeVander said the rule banning girls from boys' teams could not be waived quickly by the league and needed to be changed through its "representative process." Besides, he noted, a vote to amend that rule had been unanimously voted down at a March 24 League Representative Assembly meeting. LeVander and Donohue seemed to imply that Peggy and Toni were supposed to have asked more people earlier to make a rule change or start girls' teams. Yet the league had no intention of making a rule change, and the school districts weren't prepared to provide the two girls with teams.

At this point, the Hopkins School District attorney said he'd like Judge Lord to leave Toni out of the hearing and limit the discussion to an "immediate need in St. Cloud." O'Brien, who found himself in limbo about the Hopkins district's position, had also fallen behind on discovery. Besides, Toni's season wasn't until September. That request didn't fly with Judge Lord, who pointed out that this had all been discussed at an earlier meeting with O'Brien's legal partner.

"We had an agreement to try them together at this time," Judge Lord said. "I will deny your motion."

That is when Toni was called to testify.[2] Wexler asked her about her desire to be a member of the boys' cross-country running and skiing teams, the frequency and mileage of her workouts, whether she thought she could qualify to become a member of the boys' inter-scholastic cross-country team, and what opportunities, if any, there were for girls to participate in cross-country activities. Toni testi-fied that she had asked the Hopkins athletic director and coaches at team meets whether she could compete. They all said no. Though she worked out with the boys in cross-country running and skiing and her teammates were friendly, no one was willing to allow her to com-pete head to head and include her points in the team's score.

On cross-examination, Toni didn't like LeVander's tone or ques-tions. "It was very intimidating," she told a reporter decades later. "I was very angry with some of the questions."[3] It is hard to see from just the text, but it seems Toni heard something in LeVander's tone or saw something in his expression that made her bristle when he said, "I believe you testified that you skied along with them when they have been going cross-country, up in the woods?" She corrected him: the team practiced on a golf course. She felt he was implying that she was more interested in going off into the woods with a group of boys than training.

LeVander also asked her about practicing with the boys and par-ticipating in two meets. "I wasn't competing against the boys," Toni explained. "I was just being timed for myself."

"If the Hopkins Eisenhower High School had a girls' cross-country interscholastic team, or was going to have one this fall, you would be satisfied, wouldn't you?" LeVander asked.

"Not really, but I would compete on it," Toni replied. "The level of competition isn't as good with the girls as it is with the boys. Therefore, I would not be satisfied with the interscholastic team, but I would compete on it, seeing they wouldn't allow me to compete on the boys [team] if they had a girls' team."

Then LeVander asked what Toni had done to "inaugurate" a girls' program in either cross-country running or skiing. She said the school expected her to recruit girls to participate. "I don't see any boys doing this," she said. "And I didn't feel that it was the correct way to get a team together. So it just didn't work. We didn't have a team." She added that her mother did discuss adding girls' sports programs with the superintendent as well.

LeVander's next question seemed to be tinged with skepticism, as he asked it twice in much the same way: "What chance do you think you would have at beating a boy?" and then, "Do you think you will have a chance of actually consistently beating the boys?"

"Well, it all depends on what boy you are talking about," Toni answered. "If you are talking about the one or two best runners, probably not. We have one of the best cross-country teams in the state. But as far as the squad is concerned, I have a good chance of beating them consistently."

"Do you know how you would match up with boys from other schools? Do you have any idea?" LeVander continued.

"Yes. I would beat pretty many of them."

"Pardon?"

"I would beat pretty many of them." Toni had run and skied side by side with enough boys to know that she outperformed many of them.

LeVander took a different tack when Marie St. Pierre, Toni's mother, took the stand: "Have you done anything in the way of research, or looked into the question of what effect girls' participation on boys' athletic teams in competition would have on the health or welfare of the girl?"

"As far as my own daughter, I feel there would be no difficulty," she replied.

But certainly, LeVander contended, Mrs. St. Pierre recognized that the "average" girl could not match up with the "average" boy. Wexler objected to this statement as irrelevant; LeVander regrouped with a different question: "You would recognize, Mrs. St. Pierre, that there would be physiological differences between men and women?"

"That needs no proof," Judge Lord interjected.

"I feel, in the two years that she has been running, she has done everything with the boys, and has no ill effects, whatsoever," answered Toni's mother—who, as a nurse, would have been quite capable of expounding on the "physiological differences between men and women." She chose to focus on her daughter instead.

Much of the testimony offered by the defense focused on a generic category of female athletes. Murrae Freng, who had been named MSHSL executive director the previous year, testified that one of the "founding purposes in the League is to provide equitable competition. It just hardly seems possible that you can get equitable competition generally with girls competing against boys. The skill level there is just not the same." In fact, in his written answers to interrogatories submitted to the court, Freng had gone so far as to state that "boys are physiologically superior to girls in their high school years."[4] In court, Freng added, "Certainly if the rule was not there—it applies both ways—if the girls were permitted on boys' teams, I believe this would also mean that boys would be permitted on girls' teams." When Wexler pressed him on this point, Freng acknowledged that there wasn't a girls' team in St. Cloud for boys to join.

Yet school officials and MSHSL administrators often expressed concern about boys wanting to play on future girls' teams. St. Cloud superintendent Kermit Eastman was quoted in the *St. Cloud Daily Times* the day of the hearing:

> We are equally concerned with reverse discrimination, which could result. Should the rule be removed for girls it would seem boys would then have the right to claim the right to participate on girls' interscholastic teams.
>
> At least in certain interscholastic sports, boys could beat the girls out for team qualification. As an example, we have plans for a girls' interscholastic volleyball team this next year. Boys, with their superior height, could replace girls on their own interscholastic volleyball team.[5]

"I believe it would be a vast majority of the girls who would not be able to compete against the boys in an equitable way," Freng stated in the courtroom.

"So the rule was passed to make it possible to help the girls, in effect, wasn't it?" Judge Lord asked.

"That is correct," Freng answered.

"When it no longer works to help the girls, what do you do with it then? It looks as though it's narrowed in as to whether or not it is helping these girls or hurting them, whether it's a good and valid rule, whether it's reasonable, arbitrary, and capricious as applied to these girls at this particular stage in their life under the facts here. Then the question I have is: Is it helping these girls or hurting them?"

Freng responded, "I guess I just can't see how we can separate the two from the total."

MSHSL officials doggedly held tight to the rule's importance in protecting girls' athletics. Allowing an exception, Freng said, would result in a "step backward" for girls' athletics. But when asked repeatedly about how setting aside the rule would hurt the two girls in question, Freng could not muster an answer. "I guess I find it so difficult to separate one or two specific individuals from the total class," he reiterated.

"There is no class here," Judge Lord said. "It is only these two girls."

"If the rule is set aside for two, isn't it then logical to set aside for all?" Freng asked.

Judge Lord pushed further. "The question you were asked, the question Mr. LeVander asked you is: What would be the effect upon these two girls? Would it be in their best interests? He didn't ask you what was going to happen to the League or the schools somewhere else or to some other programs."

At this point, Wexler objected, stating that he did not think Freng was "the person who can answer the question." Freng's education and experience were in neither health nor sport. Judge Lord agreed, and Wexler's motion was sustained.

Murrae Freng had a bachelor's degree in music and a master of arts in music education. He worked for nineteen years in public schools, where he was involved in mostly music and drama. He joined the MSHSL in 1965 and became acting executive director in the fall of 1970. Wexler had called him as a witness to address the MSHSL rules, operations, and structure, not the psychological or health impacts of sport on boys and girls.

"I was thinking of it from an educational point of view," LeVander said. "I thought that was one of the functions of the educational people, to be concerned about students' health."

But Judge Lord countered, "A blind assumption that running against boys is worse for a girl's health than running against girls without some scientific evidence, is not very helpful to the Court."

At that point, Wexler asked Freng to explain what would happen if St. Cloud Tech allowed Peggy to play on the tennis team in defiance of the league rule. "They would be using an ineligible player, and as such, any games with her on the team would be forfeited," he answered. The league could even take an action as extreme as dropping the school's league membership entirely. He went on to explain that if other teams chose to compete against Tech, knowing that the school was using an ineligible player, they would be subject to the same penalties—penalties with real teeth. Losing MSHSL governance and statewide tournaments for all extracurricular activities was not something any high school administrator cared to contemplate.

After questioning MSHSL officials, Wexler moved on to a more sympathetic witness. Patrick David Lanin spelled his last name and identified himself as Toni's "coach on an informal basis" as well as the coach for cross-country running and skiing at Eisenhower High School. An avid distance runner, Lanin was well connected in the state's running community. His credentials included president of the Minnesota Association of the Amateur Athletic Union, member of the National AAU Long Distance Running Committee, and regional director for the AAU's Upper Midwest Area.

"In your opinion, can Toni St. Pierre compete favorably with any or all of the boys that are on interscholastic cross-country teams in the State of Minnesota?" Wexler asked.

"She could not compete favorably with all of the boys, but she could definitely compete favorably, I'd say, with a significant percentage on the state-wide level," said Lanin, who added later that he thought Toni belonged among the top third of the state's cross-country runners, and he considered that a conservative estimate. He also noted that his team, which included about twenty runners, had "no inability level": "Everybody that comes out and wants to run has a chance to run regardless of his ability. I don't do any cutting." He assured Wexler that he could handle additional runners—girls or boys. "The varsity team is chosen on the basis of the top seven times. That's it. It's strictly on an objective time basis."

When LeVander questioned Lanin, the exchange gradually became more and more contentious. Though Lanin had no role in initiating the actual lawsuit, he had spent two and a half years encouraging and coaching Toni, and he thought she should have a chance to run and ski with her high school teams. But even on that point, he was unwilling to concede any agreement with LeVander.

"Now, you would like to bring her over on the men's team at Hopkins, isn't that right?" LeVander asked. (For some reason, the boys' team had now become the "men's" team.)

"This isn't my wish necessarily," Lanin responded.

"Oh, I misunderstood your testimony. I gathered that you were rather favorably disposed to the idea of her coming onto your men's team in cross-country."

"I would say I would be neutral on the idea. She fits in with the team. She competes with the boys in workouts and so on. It's a rather neutral feeling."

Later LeVander would take a different tack as he questioned Lanin about his motivation for adding a girl to his team.

> LeVander: Would it be advantageous to your team to have Toni on it?
> Wexler: I object to the whole line of questioning as being irrelevant, Your Honor.
> Judge Lord: Overruled.
> Lanin: Yes, I think so.
> LeVander: So you, as a coach, would look a little better if you had her on the team because your chances of victory would be greater, is that what you are saying?
> Lanin: No.
> LeVander: That would have nothing to do with it?
> Lanin: No.
> LeVander: Notwithstanding your two years of coaching AAU?
> Lanin: No, that's not part of it.

LeVander: What is the reason that you are advocating her coming on your team?

Lanin: Because she wants to run.

LeVander: Because she wants to run.

Lanin: If anybody wants to run, they can run on my team.

Then LeVander's questioning moved on to whether schools should be expected to serve exceptional athletes. "Do you think it's educationally sound to provide special opportunities for the exceptionally gifted athletic person?" he asked.

"I think it applies in athletics as well as academics. I think the opportunity should be there," Lanin responded.

"So what you are saying is that it is the obligation of the school to provide a special facility or special program for each highly gifted individual?"

"I think we can accommodate that with the present programs that we have in the schools. I think [we can do that] if we have flexibility within our programs in the classrooms, in the physical education facilities. I think this is possible."

LeVander asked what Lanin had done to start a girls' team. Lanin explained that as a junior high science teacher, he lacked direct contact with the high school students because he worked in a different building. But he had sought to involve girls in running and skiing.

"You could run girls' events and boys' events at the same time?" LeVander asked.

"If there were other girls to compete against, yes," Lanin responded. But a girls' athletic program had not been developed in the Hopkins School District, he said. "I like to feel that our boys' program is very adequate. The girls' program doesn't exist. There isn't any girls' program."

Wexler's next witness was George Potter, St. Cloud Tech's athletic director. While Wexler had intended to call Peggy's tennis coach as well, during a recess he determined that Potter, who was present, could answer his questions as effectively as the coach, who was not on hand. Relying on a conversation he had had with the coach, Potter testified that Peggy would likely rank third or fourth on the tennis team. He explained that boys who don't qualify to play in the varsity matches still remain part of the squad. "We don't cut youngsters," he said. Potter acknowledged that Peggy had been practicing with the team and confirmed that there had been no "adverse reactions" from the boys or from Peggy.

When Wexler finished, LeVander decided to probe beyond any actual adverse reactions to any potential ones: "What, if any, problems do you see from a coach's point of view?"

"Well," said Potter, who had coached boys for eighteen years, "I would say there could be a problem in some cases with the relationship between the coach and student, so to speak. I am not sure that— well, I would say that all coaches, number one, would not want to coach girls. That is, all male coaches would not want to coach females. I am not sure that all of them would be qualified to coach females."

"Are you speaking now from an educational point of view as well as emotionally qualified?" LeVander asked.

"Well, maybe emotionally. I am not sure that all male coaches would understand females like they do males." Then LeVander led Potter to the issue of first aid and injuries. Potter said that coaches were required to have basic knowledge in the care and treatment of injuries and that while that training dealt with many common injuries, he acknowledged that he was never taught how to deal with "female injuries." "I believe this would be a problem that possibly some men could handle, and possibly some men could not handle," Potter said.

He also foresaw locker-room problems: "It would be impossible for one coach to be present in both locker rooms, no matter how you put it." He speculated that combining girls and boys on a team would entail added expense because a chaperone or second coach would be necessary "for the girls who are going to be separated from the boys inevitably at certain times."

Potter confirmed that a girls' interscholastic tennis team *might* be offered at St. Cloud Tech that fall. School district administrators had been considering girls' athletics since 1969; after three years of gathering input and further study, they had added interscholastic girls track and field, and now there was even school board approval for other sports. But nothing was certain. "May I say a qualified 'yes,'" Potter said, "depending upon the numbers . . . we have to have some competition to play against. We would certainly have to have an interest among the girls, which hopefully we will have. Hopefully we will have a girls' tennis coach or a man who is qualified to coach tennis to young ladies." In later questioning, he testified that the Minnesota Department of Education's requirements for coaching boys were different from those for coaching girls. But he noted that Tech did have personnel who would qualify to coach a girls' tennis team.

After establishing that a girls' team could be on the horizon, LeVander asked Potter to expand on yet another theoretical "adverse" impact resulting from allowing Peggy to compete on the boys' teams: "In your opinion, as an educator and Athletic Director, what would happen if this wall of separation between the two sports fields classifications were to be broken down, what would happen as far as boys being able to play on girls' teams?"

"Well, in my opinion, one of my concerns is that young men would ask and want to play on the young ladies' tennis teams," Potter said. "I think this is very possible." In fact, he continued, it might hurt the participation of both girls and boys in sports.

But Judge Lord didn't see it that way. If the court intervened on behalf of these two girls, he said, the league could adjust its eligibility system to fairly remedy the issues.

"I am terribly concerned that the Court is apparently limiting the scope of the inquiry to what is only applicable to two people," LeVander said, while "the complaint here asks this Court to set aside these rules as being unconstitutional." If the issue was that Peggy and Toni were being discriminated against because they were girls, he felt it was important to discuss the rationale for separate girls' and boys' athletics. "I don't see how we can view that in the context of only what might happen to these two people. It seems to me it has much broader implications."

Wexler noted that he had just one more witness, an administrator from the Hopkins School District, who would be available the following day. At that point, LeVander took over for the defendants,

outlining a theory for the MSHSL's case and the witnesses he intended to introduce. Judge Lord urged him to consider how much
of the testimony would be repetitive. "You shouldn't have to have
over two experts on any given facet on this case," Lord said. "When
I heard you recite the names and pedigree of all these witnesses, it
seems a little bit heavy."

"I will certainly audit them with the greatest of skill between
now and Court tomorrow," LeVander said. "And try to eliminate any
possible duplication that I can . . ."

"Well, do your best to cut it down, if you will."

LeVander opened his part of the case by calling Dorothy
McIntyre. With her credentials as a teacher and MSHSL administrator, she addressed the evolution of girls' athletic programs in
Minnesota. She gave a brief history: There had been girls' sports
programs in Minnesota on a limited basis, particularly basketball,
and some state swimming meets from 1924 to 1942. But due to criti-
cism about girls participating in sports, schools began to "backtrack,"
no longer allowing sports programs beyond the intramural level. In
the early 1950s and 1960s, spurred by weak results in the Olympic
Games, the American Medical Association and the Professional
Physical Education Association began to investigate what was happening to children's physical fitness levels in U.S. schools. "This all
culminated in the early 1950s with these new studies and the support of the American Medical Association, which decided again that
females were part of the human race, and they did indeed need exer-
cise, challenge, and stimulation," McIntyre said. "The sixties is when
we began in Minnesota to first rebuild a very solid program for girls
which would offer the opportunity for them to participate that has
been offered previously to boys."

In the early 1960s, only a few schools had any girls' sports programs with competition between schools; a "handful" had "an occasional extramural contest with other schools in the form of a Play Day
or Sports Day." As a physical education teacher, McIntyre found herself driving the team bus and organizing bake sales to finance girls'
athletics. "I served on the first gymnastics committee in the state
which, technically, originated this entire question of girls participat-

ing once again in sports programs in Minnesota," she said. "It was at that time that we discovered the severe lack of opportunity." In the 1960s, McIntyre conducted gymnastics clinics across the state for hundreds of girls, expanding their skill levels and appetite for competition. She was also involved in developing the MSHSL guidelines for girls' interscholastic athletics.

Though she was LeVander's witness, Judge Lord jumped in. "Why did you do that?" he asked. "What are the things that you thought a girl would get out of that that would make it wise to provide her with athletic activities?"

McIntyre's answer focused on both maintaining a basic level of fitness to "participate fully in life's activities" and overcoming "folklore, superstition, and myths" perpetuated by families and schools as to "what girls should do and what they should not do."

When Judge Lord asked for more elaboration, Wexler objected politely: "Excuse me, please. Your Honor, before we go any farther here, my objection to this type of questioning is going to be the same. If the Court wants to hear it, perhaps I should have a continuing objection to questions relating to girls in general and not to these particular plaintiffs."

"Well, I have conceded—and I hope wisely—to Mr. LeVander's contention that we should look at the whole picture as well as at the individual picture, whether or not what relief I might grant might be on an individual basis," Judge Lord said. "But I think I should look at the whole system and the reason for it in order to determine whether it's reasonable or unreasonable. . . . You can have a standing objection."

Quoting a recent decision in a Connecticut trial court, Judge Lord asked McIntyre for her reaction to a judge's statements about girls participating in sports: "Athletic competition builds character in boys. We do not need that kind of character in girls and women of tomorrow by the conduit of putting them in athletic competition with the opposite sex."

"I do believe that the girls need a competitive opportunity in sports as well as in their intellectual pursuit," McIntyre said. "I guess my distinction would be that I don't believe there is a difference in

areas such as intelligence, sense of humor or wit that need a delinea-
tion . . . But I do believe that in the area of physical competition . . .
that indeed the classes, to be equitable, must be separated." She asserted that combining male and female athletes into "one class"
would create "inequitable competition," pointing to speed skater
Anne Henning, the sixteen-year-old gold medalist at the 1972 Winter
Olympics. McIntyre noted that Henning's time would have placed
her twenty-first or lower in the men's event. "Now, she, as being the
best in the entire world among women, received due recognition . . .
I don't believe she would have been recognized as being twenty-first
or twenty-second." She continued: "I taught [in] high schools where
there was no program for girls outside of the intramural. I know what
that was like for my girls. So I have spent many years providing programs . . . and I believe that the only way it's going to be continued
as an equitable program is for girls to achieve success within their
level of classification. Even though their times and distances may
not be as high as men's, I do not believe it is less of a championship
performance."

At this point, a skirmish broke out over exactly what outcome
Wexler was seeking and whether the judge needed to go so far as to
strike down the rule requiring girls and boys to compete separately.
Judge Lord asked, "Wouldn't it be possible to fashion a remedy that
would give these two girls relief? . . . I want as much of this lady's information that I can get that bears on the exact decision which might
be made here, and not a broad, slashing attack upon the total constitutionality of it, but rather its impact as applied to these two plaintiffs. Plaintiff's counsel has carefully excised all of the fatty tissue
from around that particular issue, and has asked for relief for these
two people."

Wexler clarified further: "It's our position only that as to these
two plaintiffs where there is no girls' team provided, that they be
given the opportunity to try to qualify for the boys' team; and if they
can qualify, to participate just as a boy can participate on that boys'
team. I do admit, however, that it is our ultimate, but not too far removed, contention that all girls who find themselves in situations
similar to these plaintiffs, where there is no girls' team, be given the

same opportunity. But we are not asking the Court to rule on that here today."

LeVander, who argued that the rule had been drawn for all the girls and boys in the state, not two girls, interjected, "Now, I don't know any theory under which any eligibility case has ever been able to be tried in a vacuum, that it is only going to apply to two people, when you are asking to set aside the rule as being unconstitutional."

"Well, that might be one of the elements of the unconstitutionality that the Court might consider," Judge Lord said, "that it is a straight and rigid rule that makes no exception for the individual case." A rule that doesn't allow girls capable of competing with boys to do so while failing to offer any alternative "may make it unconstitutional."

"I certainly am not, at this point, sold on the theory that the total distinction between boys and girls in these programs should be knocked out," Judge Lord added. "I think that would be educationally unsound and rather infeasible. On the other hand, as applied to these two girls, that may be different."

With that, the Judge declared a recess until 10 a.m. the next morning.

The Brendens drove home that night, tired and unsure of what they had just seen. They were unaccustomed to legal proceedings and didn't really understand where the process was headed or how long it might take. They would not be returning to the courtroom for more.

5

EDUCATORS AND EXPERTS

The following morning, the newspaper headlines read "Boys to Dominate Teams If Girls Are Eligible—Freng" and "Miss Brenden to 'Suit' Up with Boys?"[1] The first highlighted the message of male superiority delivered by the Minnesota State High School League executive director; the second was weirdly provocative, as though Peggy would be dressing with her teammates. Perhaps it was just a play on words, with no ulterior meaning intended. Either way, it was likely an editor's idea of humor. The news coverage pointed out that Judge Lord had "repeatedly mentioned that he was not deciding whether the League rules must apply to all girl athletes, but only whether the two plaintiffs were entitled to relief," and that he offered "strong hints" that he may "enjoin the league from enforcing its rules against the two plaintiffs."[2]

On the second day of testimony, Thomas Wexler led with his promised witness, Hopkins athletic director George Reynolds, who over the course of the past fifteen years had served as a high school physical education instructor, assistant basketball coach, and golf coach. Reynolds confirmed that he would not allow Toni to compete with the boys' cross-country team because as a member of the MSHSL, "we have to enforce their rules." He testified that Hopkins Eisenhower was registered with the league for one girls' interscholastic sport, girls' track, new that year. The previous year the school had offered extramural girls' track. No one asked him how many sports teams existed for Hopkins boys. (The Eisenhower High School yearbook from 1972 includes twelve different boys' interscholastic sports.) Wexler asked Reynolds whether there were certain injuries that occurred more often among the girls.

"No," he answered.

"Are your boys' coaches generally required to treat the injuries that occur to their team members?" Wexler asked.

"Well, this becomes very much a case of judgment," Reynolds said. "If a person thinks that it is of a very minor nature, they may take care of it. But most injuries . . . are treated by physicians."

"Right," Wexler continued. "And you don't require or expect your coaches to practice medicine, do you?"

"Absolutely not," Reynolds replied.

With this, Wexler was finished addressing the uncomfortable issue of where and how coaches might touch girls injured during practice or competition.

Bernhard LeVander decided to find out more about girls' athletics at Hopkins Eisenhower. "You have no other interscholastic girls' programs offered up at this time?" he asked.

"No," Reynolds said.

"What is the reason for that, Mr. Reynolds?"

"I think, in our particular school district, the people involved in the Physical Education Department have discussed this at length. There's some very marked differences of philosophy within our own school district. We have people in the Physical Education Department feeling that maybe we don't want interscholastic athletics for girls at all. Some feel maybe some type of program would be desirable. We registered for the girls' interscholastic track program this year to primarily make sure that our girls could participate in an interscholastic program and also participate in the State Girls' Track Meet, if they can qualify."

"Has there been substantial interest on the part of girls manifested to get into interscholastic competition in your school?" LeVander asked.

"Oh, I think there is a very definite interest and desire on certain parties," Reynolds said. "As far as the entire total student body, no, we have no revolution going in girls' athletics."

LeVander then asked Reynolds to speculate about what would

happen to girls' athletics if the rule banning girls from boys' teams were set aside. Wexler objected, but Judge Lord, though acknowledging the answer would not be based on actual experience, overruled him. "Let's speculate about it anyway," Lord said. "What do you think it would do? . . . It helps, Mr. LeVander, for you to ask this kind of question, because it will help me to determine what, if anything, can be done here. What are the manifestations of the action that I might take? I appreciate your developing that; it saves me asking questions."

Reynolds speculated that there would be very few girls, if any, that could make boys' teams. If they participated on boys' teams, they would likely become discouraged and then might seek competition among other girls. At this point, however, his testimony took a turn LeVander probably didn't appreciate. "Deep down, when I think about this, I think the separate programs are the best route to go," Reynolds said. "But I think we have got to have time to get this process going. . . . I wish we could have a moratorium on this thing. I wish we could say for the next three years or five years, a talented girl in any sport, if she can make the boys' team, go ahead and make it, and this is going to take care of our needs of the individual talented girl, and at the same time give us ample time to work on our total program for girls." He added, "I would like to see these girls who would meet this so-called gifted category have a place to compete for a while until this girls' program can be worked out and got off the ground and going."

LeVander leaped in to claim that this would be yet another form of "reverse discrimination." If gifted girls get to play on boys' teams, he asked, wouldn't the school be discriminating against the "less talented and able girls" who do not have that opportunity?

"You might be talking about the next case that I heard is going to be brought on," Lord said. "Someone mentioned to me that they are going to bring one on for all the girls on the basis that there is more money spent on boys than girls. That might be the next case. But this one involves these two girls."

Then LeVander returned to the question of rendering first aid. "Isn't it a fact," he asked, "that a coach often does have to give first aid treatment in an emergency situation if the kid is injured before he can be taken to a doctor?"

> Reynolds: Yes.
> LeVander: And wouldn't a coach, if you have a male coach for a male team and you have a girl on it—she could get hurt, too?
> Reynolds: Sure.
> LeVander: And she could get hurt anyplace on her body, isn't that true?
> Reynolds: True.
> LeVander: And do you think it is feasible for a male coach to give her first aid any point on her body, I mean, that this is perfectly acceptable?
> Reynolds: I don't know if I am qualified to answer that.

At this point, Judge Lord chimed in: "Well, I have a couple of daughters. If they were hurt and somebody treats them that is all there is to it. I wouldn't send for a nurse."

After Reynolds, Wexler added one more witness, Charlotte Striebel, whose daughter Kathryn, had helped inspire Peggy to write to the Minnesota Civil Liberties Union. A mathematics professor at the University of Minnesota, Striebel was a feminist who fought for equity in employment, wages, and athletics. During the 1971–72 school year, she had filed a grievance with the St. Paul Human Rights Commission to allow Kathryn to swim with the Murray High School boys' swimming team. The St. Paul schools had no girls' swimming team and "zero athletic teams for girls," according to Striebel. Her twelve-year-old daughter had gained a spot on the boys' team thanks to St. Paul's sex-discrimination ordinance and an MSHSL rule that allowed schools to set their own eligibility requirements for competition within a school district. In December, however, Kathryn had been "beached by rules" when she was pulled from an event as she perched on the block waiting for the race to begin. Just the night before, she had proudly reported to her mother that she had earned a slot in the individual medley by outswimming a teammate. Now the coaches decided her participation would violate the MSHSL eligibility rule prohibiting girls from participating with boys in interscholastic athletics because the swim meet was against Irondale High School, which was in the Mounds View school district. The Irondale swim coach, who was also Kathryn's AAU swim coach, said he dared not risk his entire school's MSHSL eligibility for the next year to allow her to compete. He would not pit his team against an "ineligible" athlete. The consequences were too severe to let her race in the 400-yard freestyle with the "B" team.[3]

Charlotte Striebel felt that the MSHSL's rule was discriminatory and treated her daughter like a "second class citizen." Though she had urged Wexler to develop Peggy and Toni's case as a class-action lawsuit that would include her daughter, Wexler did not see that as a winning strategy. Apparently, however, she did convince him that she could serve as a valuable witness. LeVander objected to her testimony, arguing that it was a different situation with different facts and not material to the matter at hand. Judge Lord overruled him. Striebel testified that her daughter and other girls had swum against boys in several meets without any issues. The only small problem her daughter had encountered was the time she had to change clothes in a boiler room. "I think it has been a very good experience for her," she said.

LeVander asked whether she would want her daughter to swim on the boys' team even if a girls' team existed. Striebel responded, "If—this is a very big 'if'—if there were a girls' team that was equal to the boys' team, had the same coaching and the same competition, I would be delighted. But that doesn't happen anyplace, ever. The very best programs in the state compared to the very worst boys' programs—there is just no comparison." Upon further questioning, she added, "If there was a team that was equal in coaching and in competition, I would love to look at it and I would make the decision then. I mean, if somebody gave me a million dollars, I might accept it tomorrow, too. But that is not anything that I consider in the realm of possibility in the next three hundred years, so I really don't speculate about it much."

"So you take a very dim view of the future for girls' athletics?" LeVander asked.

"Based on the history of girls' athletics in this state, yes," Striebel replied. She thought it would be a long time before separate girls' athletic programs would match the athletic opportunities boys currently claimed.

"You do recognize a lot of work has been done, particularly in the last three years to promote and push it?" LeVander said.

"I do, yes."

"And you also recognize, do you not, that the boys' program took many years to develop it to the point where it is today?"

"In six years, my daughter will be out of school."

After Striebel finished her testimony, a recess was called. When the trial resumed, Wexler began to summarize his case:

> It is our contention that in dealing with a classification based on sex by itself that we are dealing with a suspect classification under the Fourteenth Amendment; that the burden of proof justifying that classification is on the defendants. That the basic equal protection rule is that all persons similarly situated should be treated alike unless there are substantial differences.
>
> And it occurs to me, too, that we are dealing with two elements here, not only the rule but the practice under the rule, the administration of the rule. So while it could be possible that the rule would be reasonable as applied to the bulk of persons, that the practice under the rule could still amount to a denial of equal protection to the extent that we are dealing here with teams that are for skilled players and yet are excluding equal skilled girl players.

Wexler went on to give an update of Ruth Bader Ginsburg's case on behalf of a girl who wished to play on a school tennis team in New Jersey, noting that he had spoken with someone familiar with the case the previous evening. "They settled their case on the basis that where there is a true interscholastic girls' team, then there would be no mixing of the sexes, but where there was no true interscholastic girls' team, then the school could apply to participate in a one-year pilot program, which would allow girls on the boys' teams," he recounted. The rules were adapted to allow girls to participate, and the case was still pending, awaiting the outcome of the pilot program.

In later discussion, Judge Lord asked LeVander why the MSHSL wouldn't consider a similar option. "Does the League have to be stultified by its own rules?" LeVander replied that the MSHSL did not have an "experimental rule" like New Jersey offering "provision for experimentation."

The "crucial point" that Wexler chose to emphasize from the New Jersey case was that "the measuring factor of who was entitled to participate must be determined on some basis other than solely sex." Assuming that girls can't compete with boys, even though they can compete equally, amounts to a "fundamental denial of equal protection." He cited instances in which height and weight restrictions for umpire and lifeguard positions had been struck down by the courts because they, too, amounted to employment discrimination on the basis of sex because they "excluded 99 percent of the women from both of those jobs without any relevance as to their ability to perform the jobs."

At this point, LeVander jumped in, concerned that Wexler was launching into a presentation normally saved for closing arguments. "Just a minute, counsel. Are you going to argue—are we arguing this case now, Your Honor—or is this a statement of what you are claiming?" he asked.

"Yes, this is," Wexler said. "I hope it will clarify my position in the case." Judge Lord told him to proceed.

"Well, are you going to argue twice then, is that it?" LeVander asked.

"He is not arguing to the jury anyway," said Judge Lord, known for using his discretion freely to adjust courtroom practices. "I am just trying to understand what he thinks he has here. It is all right. Go ahead."

Wexler continued, "We would be willing to stipulate that there are physical differences, functional physical differences in general, between girls and boys as they exist today. That is not to say that if girls, given the opportunity to work on their sports, won't develop to the point where they might become substantially equal. But today, there are physical differences. Some of them are functional; many of them are not. But in the interest of presenting our position to the

Court and expediting the lawsuit, we would be very willing to stipulate that there are functional differences in general, without admitting the relevancy of that in this case."

"Your Honor," LeVander said, "my concern and my feeling on this subject is this, that we are here to test the validity of a rule of separation in classification between girls and boys in athletics. Any way that you attack the validity of that rule on a constitutional basis cannot be viewed in a vacuum or in an isolated situation." He went on to note that he had "evidence" that many girls would like to participate in "men's sports," claiming that if Peggy or Toni were allowed, even temporarily, to play on boys' teams, the league knew of eighty to ninety more girls who wanted a similar opportunity. "What are we going to say to them right away? I mean, we can talk all we want about limiting this thing, but we aren't going to limit it, no matter what we do, if we tamper with the rule."

LeVander continued, "It is our position that this is not a matter that rises to the dignity of any kind of constitutional issue. . . . I don't see how there is any way, under any stretch of the imagination, that we can have a test case brought by the Civil Liberties Union to attack the validity of a rule separating girls' and boys' sports and say we are only going to do it with these two girls and it is going to have no effect on anybody else."

Michael Donohue, the St. Cloud School District's attorney, followed, urging the court to drop his school district from the case. St. Cloud Tech was abiding by MSHSL rules and following MSHSL proposals in implementing girls' athletics by "starting with intramural sports activities, leading next to extramural sports activities, and, thereafter, interscholastic sports activities," Donohue said. "The evidence has shown in this case that, number 1, there has been an extramural program provided Peggy Brenden at St. Cloud Tech already this school year; number 2, interscholastic tennis is being offered in the forthcoming school year. Insofar as the equal protection is concerned under the rules as they exist now, Peggy has been given her due . . . a tennis program has been provided her. She has had the use of it in the school year. . . . it has been shown that Peggy has received the benefits to which she is entitled."

LeVander chimed in that he thought the case should be dismissed because plaintiffs hadn't shown that the rule was "unreasonable, arbitrary and capricious, as alleged." In fact, he added, George Potter, the St. Cloud athletic director—who was one of the plaintiff's witnesses—had pointed out "a lot of problems from the standpoint of the welfare of the school district" if Peggy were permitted to play on a boys' team. J. Dennis O'Brien, attorney for the Hopkins School District, briefly added his endorsement for a dismissal. Without much explanation, the court transcript includes a parenthetical statement of "Remarks off the record" more than once during this discussion, along with the mention of a brief recess.

Ultimately, Judge Lord told all the attorneys he wasn't ready to grant any motions for dismissal without further deliberation, and so LeVander moved on to call a witness: Paula Bauck, a physical education teacher in Moorhead, Minnesota, with experience coaching girls' volleyball, gymnastics, and softball. She enthusiastically promoted girls' track and worked to create a statewide meet.[4]

Most of the witnesses who testified in that Minneapolis courtroom wanted girls to have athletic opportunities, eventually. In fact, some of them were considered champions of girls' and women's athletics. But they wanted to gradually build a separate system, drawing in girls of all abilities without altering boys' athletics. They wanted to avoid pitting girls against boys. They sought to maintain boys' sports without disruption. They feared that any exception to the rule banning girls from competing against boys might siphon away talented athletes from girls' teams, slow the development of girls' athletic programs, and allow boys to dominate the high school rosters. Sometimes they almost made it sound humiliating for girls to consider competing with boys on the same courts, tracks, or fields. Bauck explained her support for the rule separating boys and girls in athletics:

> There is a difference in the physical development of the girl and of the boy. When the girl is reaching the stage of puberty, then we have the change of the hormones, which will change her physical setup. It is at this time that the pelvic area becomes

shallow and broader and we say the girl gets hips. This in track is a definite deterrent as far as a fast runner is concerned. Those who had a definite, well, a more definite moving out of the hips will be slower runners, because the femur then sets in at an acute angle and cannot run as fast. That is just plain scientific knowledge; you can check it in any books. . . . The female has a smaller heart, and she also, therefore, has a higher pulse rate. This is just a known fact. Along with that, her breathing is very shallow, her thoracic cavity is much smaller than in the male; and when you go to track you need to have enough oxygen to last. Her recovery period is much slower than it is for a male. And to me these things are all very important as far as track is concerned.

Bauck was asked to provide comparisons between records set by girls and boys in track or in any other activity sponsored by the league. "In our high school our best girl has run 11.2 [seconds] in a 100-yard dash," she said. "This would put her maybe eighth place on the boys' team. The boys run it 9.9 and 10, 10.3, or maybe even less, you see. So our girls wouldn't have a chance there." Even if there was no girls' program, she saw no benefit in allowing girls to compete with boys: "I could see no glory for the girls. And, after all, when you are out to win, you are out to win. When you are going to set a record, for instance, as in track, you have to compete against girls to set a record, and what good would it do if you are going to go against some boys?"

"A girl competing against a boy has no chance to be a champion, is that right?" asked LeVander. Bauck agreed that was true for Moorhead's track athletes.

"Are you telling this Court that no girl has a chance to beat a boy, ever?" Wexler asked in his cross-examination.

"It would depend upon the activity," Bauck conceded. "I wouldn't know."

"It would vary from girl to girl and boy to boy, as to the capabilities of those competitors, would it not?"

"Yes. Yes, it would."

"Isn't it also true that some boys have no chance to beat other boys in certain sports because of the difference in their skill levels? Isn't it true that whether or not a girl can beat a boy depends upon the skill levels of the competitors involved?"

"The way you have asked that I would have to answer 'yes.'"

Wexler went on to ask whether there were other qualities necessary to capably perform in athletics besides the factors that Bauck had stated earlier. He proceeded to list a series of physical and mental abilities—body control, mental determination, courage, concentration, analytical ability, quickness, eyesight, hearing, timing, poise, and grace. "Do you know if the capacity of boys in all of those elements exceeds the capacity of girls?" he asked.

"I guess right now I would have to be unsure," Bauck said.

"In light of the characteristics that we have just discussed, is it your opinion that boys are always more qualified than girls?" Wexler asked in a restatement of the question.

"No," Bauck answered.

"And wouldn't it in fact be your opinion that some boys, because of their physical development, will never be able to compete with other boys in certain sports?"

"Yes."

LeVander's next witness was Lars Kindem, a Norwegian language and American history teacher who coached track and skiing at Roosevelt High School in Minneapolis. Kindem worked for the United States Ski Association (USSA), serving as chairman of cross-country for the central United States and as a member of the committee governing "Junior Nordic Competition" and the "Ladies Technical Committee for Cross Country." He testified that neither the National Collegiate Athletic Association nor the Olympics permitted women to compete on men's teams or men on women's teams.

"Is there in the Olympics any special test given for a woman to determine whether she is in fact a woman before permitting her to compete in the Olympics?" LeVander asked.

Kindem explained that a "so-called sex control test" was given because Communist Bloc countries allegedly injected women with steroids, which resulted in masculine characteristics and increased athletic performance levels. He added that no such test was administered to men. LeVander asked Kindem for his opinion, based on his experience as a coach and educator, of "mixing the sexes in interscholastic competition."

"I don't believe they should be mixed," Kindem answered. He said he based his response on his attempt to start the first girls' ski team in Minnesota the preceding winter. More girls than boys had appeared at the start, and when they worked out together, "sometimes the boys and sometimes the girls got a little silly. They were self-conscious. Sometimes they had fun." After some time, he said, about a third of the girls dropped out; a short time later, another third dropped out. The girls did not compete against the boys. Kindem set up a racing schedule for the girls to compete against girls from three other high schools. It's not clear whether his opinion about mixing the sexes was based on his experience with the girls' dropout rate, the "silliness," or some other factor.

LeVander then asked how Toni would "stack up with the boys." Kindem, citing official USSA race records from 1972, compared Toni's race times with other girls and boys. He pointed to 5-kilometer races in January and February and compared her times with boys racing the same course; though she had placed first and second among the girls, she would have been thirteenth and eighteenth among boys. However, the comparisons were not head-to-head competition and involved competitors of different ages. In USSA junior ski events, boys skied 10 kilometers while girls were limited to skiing 5 kilometers. Kindem conceded that Toni was better than "some" seventeen-year-old high school boys, but he doubted it was a lot.

LeVander later asked Kindem of Toni, "In your opinion, would it be in her best interest from a physical, emotional, and, let's say, a psychological point of view for her to play or to take part in a boys' cross-country ski team . . . ?"

"I am not sure it would be an advantage for her," Kindem said. Upon further questioning, however, he admitted he did not have any basis for thinking there was anything "harmful" about mixed competition and said he thought Toni "should continue." It's not clear what that meant.

Belmar Gunderson, assistant professor and chairman of the intramural and extramural sports program for women at the University of Minnesota, was LeVander's next witness. (The University of Minnesota did not form a women's intercollegiate athletics department until 1975; Gunderson led it.) She had a PhD in physical education and an extensive history of participation in national professional organizations connected to women in sport, health, physical education, and recreation. Her credentials were so voluminous that Judge Lord eventually asked LeVander to move on from reciting them. A former amateur tennis player who competed at Wimbledon, winner of multiple doubles championships, and coauthor of an article with Billie Jean King, Gunderson had substantial knowledge and experience in building athletic opportunities for women. She testified that she was sympathetic to Peggy and Toni.

"I want these girls to have opportunities in sports, and I think the State of Minnesota is way behind in offering these opportunities, but I think to ask the girls to compete against guys to win a spot on the team is the wrong way to do it," she said.

"Why do you say that?" LeVander asked.

"Because they cannot compete. They can't do it," Gunderson replied. "Their strength—they are not as strong, they are not as tall, they don't have the same muscle mass. It's just not a fair contest. And I think all of us in sport like to see fairness or equality in sport. And it will take a while to develop women's programs."

Judge Lord pointed out that previous testimony had shown Peggy could make the team and compete successfully.

"Right," Gunderson said. "She is competing with mediocre boys probably. I don't know. I haven't seen them. I haven't seen her play."

Lord went on to ask what "damage" would result by having a girl play on a boys' team.

"I can't answer whether or not it is going to damage the girl," Gunderson said. Her concern was not for an individual girl but about the development of girls' athletics overall. "I do think the fact that they allow her to play on the boys' team will give that institution or that school board an opportunity to say, 'Well, this is what we are going to do for you. Any girl that wants to can try out for the team.'"

The next expert, Robert Carl Serfass, an assistant professor in the University of Minnesota's department of physical education for men, reinforced Gunderson's assertions about the physiological differences between men and women. He went into some depth describing the scientific studies documenting differences in men's and women's muscle mass and their ability to utilize oxygen for energy. When LeVander asked his opinion of the MSHSL rule, he said he did not think it should be changed. "There is no doubt about the fact that any particular girl can beat some boys," said Serfass, who was not a coach. But he did not think a "particular girl" should compete against boys. "She is not going to beat very many that are sincere about training at all. She will beat boys who are on teams who don't do very much work to train." He also noted that girls who were allowed to compete with boys would have a big edge when they "drop back into strictly female competition." "The advantages to them are tremendous," he said.

LeVander asked whether competing with boys was "desirable from a health standpoint, urging Serfass to discuss the "possibility of overtaxing" girls. Serfass was no help on that topic: "To my knowledge, no normal individual who is normally motivated ever dropped dead or had any serious impairment because of a highly competitive skill level situation. In other words, I don't think it would hurt anybody physically." When asked more specifically about a hypothetical situation that mirrored Peggy's, Serfass said he did not believe a girl playing tennis against boys would suffer any "physiological harm," He stipulated that he was only speaking of noncontact sports like tennis or running.

Serfass was the last witness of the day. The court recessed until 9:30 the next morning. Neither Peggy nor my parents received any updates on the proceedings. They simply waited.

6

IN CLOSING

"Physiology May Defeat Girls," read the headline of the next day's front-page story in the *St. Cloud Daily Times*. The article recounted that experts had "stressed that girls have inherent physiological differences that make it impossible for them to compete with boys on an equal basis."[1] The *Minneapolis Tribune* offered a similar account: "In addition to obvious characteristics of strength and height, the average male has a greater oxygen-carrying capacity that gives him more endurance, a higher hemoglobin red cell count and a larger heart size, the witnesses said. . . . Among the expert witnesses who testified yesterday were Paula Bauck, Moorhead girls' track coach; Dr. Belmar Gunderson, chairman of the women's intramural program at the University of Minnesota; and Dr. Robert Serfass, a professor of physiology and anatomy at the university."[2] The *Minneapolis Star* closed with the professor's testimony: "Serfass said a well-trained, talented girl would 'beat some boys who are average or below or who haven't trained,' but he felt there was no danger that girls 'are going to invade boys sports in large numbers.'"[3]

The news coverage focused on the expert witnesses' preference for separate athletic competition by gender because they believed, on average, girls' bodies lacked the strength and speed of boys. The stories did not address the absence of opportunities for girls, but rather the inherent limitations that prevented girls from fairly sharing games and sports with boys. The articles did not discuss the many boys who lacked the strength, speed, or skills to compete successfully with other boys or girls, nor did they take note of witnesses' assurances that the two girls in question would not be "damaged" or hurt by competing against boys.

The newspapers and witnesses never addressed the benefits Peggy and Toni would forgo if banned from existing high school athletic teams. No one discussed how the girls might be affected by the absence of competitive athletic opportunities. They didn't examine the skill development and fitness that accompanies the challenge of competition, the relationships teammates build, or the lifetime networks they create. Nor did they mention the personal and emotional growth engendered by sports programs, regardless of an athlete's skills or gender. And of course, because we were talking about two girls, there was no mention of missed college athletic scholarships. Those just didn't exist.

Elsewhere in the same April 26, 1972, edition of the *St. Cloud Daily Times* was a brief, three-inch story highlighting one of two varsity matches played by the unbeaten "Tech netmen" that week.[4] Tech gave Wayzata a "whitewashing" and upset a "sixth-rated" Brainerd 4–1. Peggy's potential season of team action was shrinking fast.

Sometimes it felt as though everyone had lost track of Peggy and Toni themselves as the plaintiffs in the case. The defense kept pointing out that it was really about the undoing of the future of girls' sports programs and that these two girls, with all their inherent physiological weaknesses, needed to accept the process and timetable that the Minnesota State High School League and school districts had in mind for their gender. The MSHSL was quite willing to look past Peggy and Toni (and the eighty to ninety girls who apparently wanted a similar opportunity). Someday there would be girls' athletic programs, and these two girls shouldn't rush the timing, join boys' teams, or alter the rules.

Toni, her mother, and her brother Sam traveled to the federal courthouse in Minneapolis for all three days of the hearing. Sam, a sophomore, sat begrudgingly through two and a half days of testimony; Toni and her mother, Marie, were keenly interested. Having watched Toni diligently train over the course of two years only to be barred from high school competition, Marie St. Pierre had initiated the case in the first place. She was the one who called the Minnesota

Civil Liberties Union and asked for help. Toni likely urged her on. "I feel it's got to be done," Toni said. "Girls have to get in there and fight."[5]

The MSHSL blamed Patrick Lanin for the court challenge. In fact, at a coaches meeting, he was greeted with expletives by a league executive, who berated him for pulling the strings to instigate Toni's lawsuit. "I didn't put her up to that," Coach Lanin tried to explain. "I didn't have anything to do with it."

"It was when I got my subpoena to appear in court that I first heard about Toni's case," he said. He told Toni that while he supported her 100 percent, he was angry she hadn't trusted him enough to tell him her plans. Toni said she figured Lanin would have been mad if he *had* known about her plans, so she didn't fill him in. She was moving ahead with her fight, regardless of her coaches' opinion.

In court, both Lanin and Toni bristled under Bernhard LeVander's questioning, which involved repeatedly demanding proof of Toni's ranking and skill. The premise: if she wasn't the very best, she probably shouldn't compete with boys—no matter that any boy, regardless of skill level, could show up for the same team and have a chance to develop his skills. Toni did not like the attorney's tone, and she felt he insinuated that her interest in Eisenhower athletics was more about male companionship than running. She would later ask Lanin what the word *protégé* meant because she thought LeVander made the word sound dirty when questioning a witness about her relationship with her coach.

As day three of the trial opened, LeVander asked Dorothy McIntyre of the MSHSL to tell the court just what would happen if the two girls were able to play on boys' teams. "Would this in your opinion also open up the avenue for boys to play on girls' teams in these same sports?" he asked.

"Objection," Thomas Wexler said, noting that the question required the witness to apply the law and interpret its impact.

"Sustained," Judge Lord ruled. "You are speculating as to what the Court might order, and the Court hasn't made any order yet. It is a legal conclusion based upon no facts."

LeVander said he thought it was important for the Court to have

the "benefit of some expertise" on the question of what might happen "if this wall of separation, as we say, is breached. In other words,
would it entail the possibility that boys could play on girls' teams if
girls could play on boys' teams?"

"It is speculation," Judge Lord said. "Proceed."

LeVander took a different tack. He read aloud a letter dated April
18, 1972, addressed to MSHSL assistant director Orv Bies. It came
from Rich Olson, the Virginia (Minnesota) High School athletic
director. In a state full of Olsons, his name would be instantly rec-
ognizable to Minnesota sports fans. In 1960, he coached the tiny
Edgerton High School's boys' basketball team to a historic one-class
state basketball title, a *Hoosiers*-style legend. In the letter, Olson in-
quired about what to do, just in case some hypothetical boy asked to
participate in an upcoming girls' track meet: "On May 13, 1972, we
are hosting the girls' qualifying meet for our area. What procedure
should we follow if this would happen?"

Girls across Minnesota were anticipating their first-ever MSHSL-
sponsored state track meet, which was coincidentally happening
as the boys marked five decades of state track-and-field meets. It is
easy to imagine that organizers would encounter plenty of questions
about this uncharted event. Olson raised no concerns about girls'
eligibility—only a red flag about a nameless boy who might suddenly
emerge at the end of the season, demanding a chance to run in a girls'
qualifying meet. "With girls wanting to participate on boys' teams,
we think this could happen in reverse, and looking ahead we wonder
how we should handle this," he wrote.[6] Wexler again objected, and
Judge Lord agreed that neither this hypothetical situation nor the
letter McIntyre wrote in response had any "probative value."

With Dorothy McIntyre on the stand, LeVander asked many
questions about athletic eligibility rules. She ticked off criteria such
as age, residence, grade level, attendance, and passing a physical examination. Judge Lord was interested in scholastic requirements.
"Any boy that can stay in school is eligible under the High School
League rules, isn't he?" he asked. McIntyre explained that student
athletes must pass a certain number of classes. While the judge challenged the academic rigor required of athletes, McIntyre responded

by explaining that athletic participation is a privilege but also serves as an inducement for students to strive for passing grades, encouraging them to keep trying. LeVander then asked her opinion on "setting aside the rules against mixed sex teams."

"I believe that setting aside the rules which establish girls' programs would set aside girls as first-class citizens," McIntyre answered. "At this point our programs provide for performance of girls at a first-class level, where they perform like a girl and as a girl. They can laugh and cry like a girl if they wish, and I note that those are not always qualities which coaches like to see in their present boys' teams."

Wexler objected yet again: "I would like to strike from the record the comment about what coaches like to see in boys as being hearsay and without foundation."

Judge Lord responded, "The court will take judicial notice of the fact that if a boy cried, he would probably be kicked off the team."

McIntyre continued: "I believe that setting aside a girls' program will force our talented girls, and particularly girls such as those in question here, to become, if I might call it, oatmeal and sausage, to fill out the spaces on a boys' team, to become the means of earning a few additional points so that their male counterparts can score the records and score the team victories . . . I do not believe that we should put our skilled girls such as Toni and Peggy into a position where they and all of the other girls in the state in a similar situation must come with full credentials in order to even try out for a team."

LeVander asked McIntyre, as an educator and an MSHSL administrator, whether she thought it was in Peggy's best interests to be allowed to play on a boys' team. "I do not believe that she has an equitable opportunity to achieve and to succeed in it, and for that reason I believe that she is being relegated to a fourth-seeded citizenship as a member of that team," she said. "I believe that on the testimony of the physiologist, it becomes evident that [Peggy's] achievement cannot be at the same level as her supposed counterparts. And the Court indicated at one point that she should go to the team to play as a boy, and I do not believe as an educator that our girls should go into boys' teams to play as a boy."

"Now, that was your opinion, and you are entitled to that," Judge Lord said. "For what help it is, I will consider it. However, in the light of the girls' alternative, you would say that she should not compete at all. I am talking about today, Peggy Brenden in St. Cloud, and she wants to compete. Now you are saying that because she might fail she shouldn't even have the opportunity to compete, aren't you?"

McIntyre answered simply, "Yes, sir."

LeVander noted that Peggy's tennis experience was already beyond the norm for most students and participating on the girls' extramural program in the fall along with interscholastic participation in the spring would be unusual for any student, boy or girl. "If Peggy plays at St. Cloud on a boys' team this year, in your opinion would this require a Betty or a Pearl or someone else similarly skilled in a special sport to be given the same opportunity either this year or next year?" LeVander asked McIntyre.

Wexler objected. Judge Lord sustained the objection, asking, "How does she know? How can she guess any better than you and I?"

That did not change the direction of LeVander's questions. He wanted McIntyre to discuss the effect of Peggy's participation on the development of girls' tennis in St. Cloud and at other schools.

"Your Honor, I am going to object to that on grounds of foundation," Wexler said. "There has been a lot of junk in this record based on exactly this same kind of speculation."

Only a few minutes later, after asking McIntyre whether it was in Toni St. Pierre's "best interest" to participate with the boys' teams, LeVander again asked, "What affect would mixing teams have in your opinion on . . . girls' sports programs?" Wexler again objected.

"One of the problems is that you add speculation on speculation . . . Mr. LeVander," Judge Lord said. "The Court here under these circumstances will probably not consider what might happen at Virginia, Minnesota, at another time, under other circumstances, but, rather, will narrow its decision to whether or not as applies to these two girls there is a sufficient interest, a sufficient reason, to discriminate against them, and if sex—it being the only reason—doesn't constitute an improper classification under the Fourteenth Amendment." He went on: "So much of this testimony as to what might happen to the total program, whether the High School League serves a good or bad purpose, whether the schools have or have not set up other programs for girls, are actually beyond the scope of our inquiry as it has now been narrowed."

McIntyre jumped in at one point, seeking a chance to share her take on what the "real issue" was before the court. She said the case was about whether boys and girls should be in separate classifications. She resented the notion that it would be a "great big favor" to let skilled girls join boys' teams. "I object to that," she said. Judge Lord did not dwell on her interpretation of the case, however, and suggested that she wait to see what the court ordered and then consult with her lawyer about the ramifications.

It wasn't long before LeVander was asking McIntyre what problems she might foresee in scheduling "mixed teams." As she spoke about the complexities of scheduling girls' teams, boys' teams, and mixed teams, she seemed to find the topic overwhelming. "It befuddles my mind at the moment," she stated. Wexler broke in, attempting to object—to which Judge Lord retorted, "You are about five minutes too late."

LeVander then began questioning McIntyre about the differences between girls' and boys' track records. He wanted to offer up high school records that would show the fastest boys' time and the fastest girls' time.

"I think that for the purposes here we can conclude that the average boy can defeat the average girl, and it is only the exceptional girl that can compete," Judge Lord said. "Do you need any more evidence on that now?" Lord then asked Wexler whether the statement he had just made was a "concession" that went too far.

"For purposes of this lawsuit, it is not too far, Your Honor," replied Wexler. "The only qualification I would make is that as of this time, as of now."

Wexler embarked on a multipronged cross-examination of McIntyre. In a rather extended and frustrating exchange, the pair addressed the subject of "equitable competition." McIntyre said that establishing equitable competition was the whole point of the league's rules. "Within sports, it's one of our biggest objectives, to provide rules which give everyone an opportunity and thereby achieving to their level of success," she said. Wexler tried to get her to acknowledge that equitable competition could exist between genders, and at the same time inequitable competition could exist among girls or among boys. He asked whether the large proportion of men who were famous musicians indicated that men make better musicians than women, or whether Black golfers should be placed in a separate class since most of the top golfers were white. McIntyre did not care to weigh in on these subjects.

"In your opinion, isn't one of the obvious competitive advantages that boys have today over girls the fact that society provides them with many athletic activities at younger ages and encourages such activities more so than they do for girls?" Wexler asked.

"That is true," McIntyre replied. "Because we are in that intermediary time when we are just beginning to recognize girls as human beings." She testified that athletic opportunities were equally important to girls as they were to boys, and athletic talents should be equally encouraged and recognized. But the only path she could see to making that happen involved creating separate but equal programs. She could not imagine allowing any girls to compete with boys even if that were the only way to give them access to athletic opportunities. McIntyre remained consistent—she argued that the rule had to apply to Peggy and Toni because they were girls. Their skill level did not matter. The absence of a girls' team did not matter. Girls should not compete with boys. It was a tautology that would be repeated over and over. The rule didn't allow for any exceptions. In one of many frustrated exchanges between Judge Lord and McIntyre, this struggle was articulated.

> Lord: My question is: These exact girls in these exact situations which you have heard here, can you figure out any justification for the rule that prohibits them from participating merely because they are girls?
>
> McIntyre: Yes. My justification is that as girls they should have the chance to compete in a similar program in St. Cloud that should have been set up there long ago.

Lord: All right. Now, the answer then is that St. Cloud should
   have done something. But today the girls are there and today
   they are able to compete, and the reason they are not able
   to compete is because the rule says that a girl can't compete.
   Now, can you think of any reason why today this Court
   should enforce that rule? Is there any justification for the rule?

McIntyre: Yes, because it does apply to more than Peggy and
   Toni.

Lord: I asked about Peggy and Toni. If you will please try to be
   helpful and we will get to the answer. As to Peggy and Toni,
   can you think of any reason why that rule is justified as to
   them?

McIntyre: Yes, because they should be competing within their
   classification.

"She fought like a tiger," Lord later said of McIntyre. "I've never
had a witness I felt more like punching in the nose."

By the time LeVander moved on to direct examination of MSHSL
executive director Murrae Freng, Judge Lord's patience was flagging.
After Freng testified in some detail about his duties and responsibilities, LeVander asked him to recount a history of the league. Judge
Lord found that more than he could bear.

"Of what relevance will that be to this narrow question?" he
snapped. "I have read the book. It's in evidence. I have read the history of the League. I have read of the former Board of Directors, the
present Board of Directors, past members. I think I can take notice of
what is in the book, if that is helpful to you." Not long after, Lord fired
off a similar question, challenging LeVander to explain the relevancy
of his line of questioning. The judge did not appreciate the detailed
discussion of the league's organizational structure, descriptions of
procedural steps, and school districts' representation. What he really
wanted to know was how LeVander would characterize the legal status of the league rule that was central to the case. "Do you regard it
to be the same as a state statute? Do you regard it to be the same as
a rule of an administrative agency on which they have hearings and
the rules are promulgated? What do you regard it to be?" he asked.

"Your Honor, we regard these rules as being the internal rules of a voluntary association of the schools of the State of Minnesota who have joined and are members of this association," LeVander answered.

"I want to get that down," Judge Lord said. He later made it clear that he wanted to know more about eligibility rules—how they are adopted, their statewide impact, and whether they would be considered a state action.

Freng addressed the rule-making process and noted that it was not "unusual for rules of the League to be contested." In fact, a citizen committee had undertaken a comprehensive study of the league's regulations and method of operation the previous year. The committee had developed a set of nearly fifty recommendations, including substantial changes in the league's articles of incorporation and constitution as well as its rules, nearly all of which had been adopted the previous spring, according to Freng. Wexler objected. Without the actual committee report on record, there was not adequate foundation for this testimony.

"If you want to bring it in, I will bring it in," LeVander offered.

"It is surplusage anyway," Judge Lord said. "I think we are going to have to zero right in on the rule and the effect on these circumstances."

Freng was asked what the league meant by equity of competition and how it went about addressing that objective. He said the league sought to set a "starting base" for students and schools that might best equalize competition. For example, it established rules for season lengths, the number of games or matches a team played, age requirements, and amount of play allowed. It also created classes of competition to provide more opportunities for tournament experiences and to make competition more equitable for schools of different sizes. In fact, Freng said, the next year the league was going to create three classes by school size for boys' track and five classes for football.[7] Schools were expected to abide by these eligibility rules and enforce them, LeVander added.

"As it applies to these two young ladies, the rule is enforced by the local school authorities who do so out of fear of being expelled or otherwise punished by this voluntary association; isn't that right?" Judge Lord asked.

"Yes, I would say that is right," LeVander said. Freng agreed.

After a recess for lunch, LeVander called Barbara Yost to testify. She was a physical education and health teacher at Harding High School, where she had recently begun serving on a St. Paul school district athletic advisory council. Yost's testimony was relatively brief. She explained that she had been elected, along with a "junior high school woman representative," to serve as a voice for St. Paul women on the twelve-member St. Paul Athletic Administrative Council. Asked at their first meeting to present a plan regarding their needs for the next year's program, the two women decided to send a survey to the "rest of the physical education women in the system." One of the questions asked was "Do you approve of girls on boys' interscholastic teams?" Yost shared the results: twenty-three no, two yes, and one no answer. Wexler asked to review the surveys. Not finding any comments or explanations with the responses, he asked Yost whether she had been given any reasons for the responses. She couldn't recall any.

Wexler objected to the survey testimony. The judge said he would allow it to "stand for what it represents." Directing his comments to the witness, Lord explained, "That is not an insult to you. What I am really saying is that this is a long way from a scientific survey."

LeVander's last witness was Sigurd Ode, assistant commissioner for the Minnesota Department of Education. Ode explained that he served as the supernumerary for the commissioner at MSHSL board of directors meetings, sitting in for the commissioner at roughly a third of the meetings. Upon questioning, he quoted the Minnesota statutes on "physical and health education instruction" and "extracurricular activities of independent school districts." Although he later corrected himself after misstating the numbering for the Minnesota statutes—126.02 and 123.38 (1971)—he seemed very confident in his interpretation.

Ode also freely defined terms and parsed the language. "May I, Mr. Counsel, Your Honor, bring out the meaning of the word 'participate,'" he expounded. "Participate means to have or take a share with others in some activity as compared to the word 'compete' which means to strive in opposition, to vie." He noted that Minnesota Statute 126.02 made participation in a physical education program compulsory, in contrast to his understanding of Minnesota Statute 123.38, which involved extracurricular activities such as school sports. "There is no compelling need for this," Ode said. "It depends on available funds." In an exchange with Judge Lord, Ode argued that state laws prevented him from supporting girls competing with boys.

"But as to these girls, at this time, can you give any valid reason as to these girls, why they should be excluded merely because they are girls?" asked Judge Lord. "You don't concede or contend that because these girls are in education they should have any less rights under the Constitution than they would have in any other governmental function, do you?"

Ode responded, "I thought, Your Honor, that I spelled this out with school law when I read the—I forget the exact number here now . . . that this was required for participation but not for competition."

Judge Lord changed his question: "You really cannot see any major objective that would be accomplished by the state in keeping these girls out merely because they are girls?"

"Again, Your Honor, I would have to say I cannot see them competing with boys.

"Why?"

"Because of Minnesota Statute 126.02, that says 'participate' and not 'compete.'"

"We are dealing here with a higher law than the Minnesota law, the United States Constitution," Lord replied, "which says that there should be equal treatment by the law."

"And I firmly advocate that, Your Honor," Ode said. But he felt that allowing girls to compete against boys would be "contrary to what I am ordained to do as a state employee."

"Well, thanks," Judge Lord said. "And, Mr. Ode, I know that you appreciate that I am not arguing with you or putting you down. I make these inquiries to really try and determine what background, what reason, what logical distinction exists to justify this kind of exclusion based on sex."

A page from Peggy
Brenden's scrapbook
features clippings from
the official handbook
of the Minnesota
State High School
League. Peggy Brenden
collection.

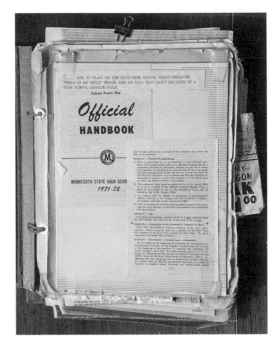

The author *(right)* with
Peggy Brenden in front of
their home in St. Cloud,
Minnesota, 1972. Sheri
Brenden collection.

The campus of St. Cloud Tech high school in 1946, with the tennis courts at lower left. Courtesy of Stearns History Museum, St. Cloud, Minnesota.

Toni St. Pierre trains for a race in 1972. Photograph by Earl Seubert; copyright 1972 Star Tribune.

Judge Miles Lord in 1976. Photograph by Kent Kobersteen; copyright 1976 Star Tribune.

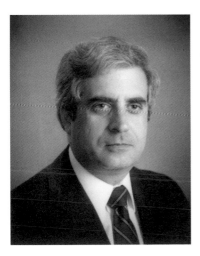

Thomas Wexler, circa 1990s. Wexler volunteered his services to the Minnesota Civil Liberties Union in representing Peggy Brenden and Toni St. Pierre. Courtesy of Hennepin County Library.

Bernhard LeVander, circa 1990s. LeVander represented the Minnesota State High School League in the case. Courtesy of the American Swedish Institute.

MONTAGE

Vol. 2, No. 8   TECHNICAL HIGH SCHOOL, ST. CLOUD, MN. 56301   May 24, 1972

Peg Brenden-From Court to Court

Peggy Brenden's legal challenge to the Minnesota State High School League was profiled extensively in the St. Cloud Tech high school newspaper. Peggy Brenden collection.

Pat Lanin's Hopkins Eisenhower cross-country teams were known to seek out unusual settings to pose for the yearbook cameras. In this photograph from 1973, Toni St. Pierre sits in the top left window of an abandoned farmhouse. Courtesy of Hennepin County Library.

A spread from the 1972 Hopkins Eisenhower yearbook featuring the boys' cross-country team, coached by Pat Lanin *(seated, right page)*. Toni St. Pierre is in the photograph above Lanin but is notably absent from the team roster. Courtesy of Hennepin County Library.

The 1973 Hopkins Eisenhower cross-country ski team. *Left to right:* Gary Lee, Toni St. Pierre, Mark Saufferer, Don Lee, Dave Lorenzen, Rod Chelberg, Mark Larson, and Sue Schaefer *(in front).* Courtesy of the Minnesota Historical Society.

The 1973 Hopkins Eisenhower girls' track team, coached by Paul Bengtson *(second from right).* Toni St. Pierre is in the back row, seventh from right. Courtesy of Hennepin County Library.

Peggy Brenden competes against Steve Krause at Coon Rapids, May 6, 1972. Photograph by Regene Radniecki; copyright 1972 Star Tribune.

Tennis champion Billie Jean King signs an autograph for Senator Walter Mondale at a hearing for Mondale's Women's Educational Equity Act in November 1973. Courtesy of the Minnesota Historical Society.

"I hope I am not evasive with you, Your Honor," Ode said. "But how pleased I am, as an educator, that we have now organized in the State of Minnesota such a fine program for high school girls' athletics under the leadership of Miss McIntyre . . . one of the best of all fifty states. We should be proud of that, grateful for it. This challenge that has come to us should have come, and justifiably so, ten years ago, when we had no program. The girls were short-changed. My, but they were short-changed! Now, they are not!"

"What have you done for Miss Brenden in tennis or for the other girl, Antoinette, in running or cross country skiing is the question?" Judge Lord fired back. It was not a question that Ode ever answered.

When Ode finished his testimony, LeVander rested his case and then gave the floor to Michael Donohue, the attorney representing the St. Cloud school district. Donohue opened by identifying a "collateral issue in this lawsuit, and that is one of inviting litigation and supporting causes that are dramatic in appeal but not of that serious import to have that standing to involve the public expenditure that is being made in this trial."

"We have and will show that our district is proceeding to fulfill and meet the needs of girls, and it has been shown that the League has done this as well," Donohue said. "It bothers me that should Peggy be afforded relief on the mere fact, as it seems, that we have not moved fast enough for her, we open the door to anyone to come in and question the speed of local government in administering the proper needs of its constituents." He asked the judge to dismiss the case. The motion was denied.

Donohue called Charles Sell Sr., principal at St. Cloud Tech, to be sworn in. Sell, who was in his third year as principal, had been a teacher for twenty-one years as well as a coach and athletic director. He testified that he served on a committee that consisted of the principals and athletic directors from the St. Cloud School District's two high schools, which had begun "looking into girls' interscholastic athletics" after an MSHSL meeting during the 1969–70 school year. Following the MSHSL recommendations, the committee first sought to build intramural and extramural athletic programs for girls. It also surveyed other schools to see which ones within the region might provide competition. Shortly before the trial began, the committee had submitted a report to the school board requesting the authority to add eight girls' sports.

"Is it proposed that the various activities for girls this coming year be run at separate times, separate from the boys'?" Donohue asked.

Sell said that to make the most efficient use of facilities, the schools would like to have boys' and girls' programs in different seasons, making gym space, tennis courts, and athletic fields easier to schedule. Seeing where this logic could lead, Lord chimed in, "Have you given any thought to running boys' tennis in the wintertime and giving the tennis courts to the girls, or running the boys' basketball in the fall and let the girls play basketball during the regular season?" Almost immediately, he added, "We should just strike that, I am only kidding you."

Lord knew the possibility of pushing boys' sports out of their traditional seasons for girls' programs was laughable. Donohue pointed out that since football and basketball game receipts were sources of funding, schools wouldn't want to do anything that might hurt ticket sales. Lord's comment, however, sprang from insight: he was beginning to see all the ways girls were being kept from participating in interscholastic athletics. Schools claimed they lacked funds; they lacked student interest; they lacked facilities and equipment; they lacked competitors. But these arguments had not hindered the growth and expansion of boys' programs. "I, myself, am learning a great deal as we go through this case about what has been happening to the girls," Lord said. "When the case first came about, I took it rather lightly, but the further you get into it, the more you realize the girls have a problem."

Donohue saw problems, too—problems he felt were serious and insurmountable. Although at least two other witnesses had addressed the "problem," he wanted Sell to discuss "rendering medical care to girls." Sell explained that as a coach, he had typically treated muscle cramps by massaging an athlete's knotted muscle. He worried about what coaches would do if that meant massaging a girl's thigh.

Judge Lord said he thought a male coach could treat a common athletic injury without touching any vital portions of a girl's anatomy.

He even gave his own home remedy for a charley horse: press on the knee and pull the heel. Donohue didn't think it was that simple; he said a coach confronted with an injured girl would be "faced with the dilemma of treating the injury and incurring social intimidation" or leaving the girl in pain.

"Every teacher makes that choice in his classroom every day," Judge Lord retorted. "I don't regard it as an important, valid consideration." If an injury is serious, he said, call a doctor. "Tennis courts aren't that far from civilization."[8]

Before the case closed, Toni returned to the stand one last time. She offered a few details about her times and placement in competitive events, testifying that she had only started cross-country skiing in December 1971. Then she commented on one last subject: having heard other witnesses' testimony about the physical advantages afforded boys, Toni wanted to share her own view about what makes a successful, competitive athlete. "It has been mentioned quite a bit about gifted people, people who are gifted in this sport, a highly gifted person is more privileged . . . and I don't think that it is gifted," she said. "In running cross-country or in skiing . . . it is something that you work out. You have to work at it. Anybody can just go out and run, but it takes a lot of work in order to be able to run cross country and to be able to compete well in it."

In closing remarks, LeVander argued that a school's decision to furnish and sponsor a sports program was "strictly discretionary." If the two girls were granted the chance to join boys' teams, the court would essentially be finding that there is a constitutional right to compete in an interscholastic activity, "which would be precedent-setting in and of itself in terms of the case law." "This would mean that the girls have a constitutional right to compete on fourteen potential boys' teams, in football, basketball, or any of these sports," opening the possibility for girls to join contact as well as noncontact teams, LeVander said.

Donohue blamed Peggy and our parents for failing to take a role in building a girls' athletic program, stating they had "made no attempt within the district to get interscholastic girls' tennis going, made no attempts whatsoever other than becoming a party to a lawsuit which commenced four days prior to the season of tennis." He continued, "Is the law going to allow one person to enter a court room because we have not moved fast enough for her, particularly when that person did nothing, did nothing whatsoever, other than in fact little more than lending her name to a lawsuit and involving the school district, the taxpayers of our area in legal fees?"

The Hopkins School District's attorney offered no witnesses, evidence, or final arguments. Quiet for most of three days, J. Dennis O'Brien seemed to be in legal limbo. The six-man Hopkins School Board, which he was supposed to represent, was of two minds. In a board meeting held as the case was heard, three members supported a motion calling the MSHSL rule discriminatory and three opted for a "neutral" position; superintendent George "Jack" Greenawalt thought a neutral position was best because he did not wish to "injure the relationship between the district and the league." This split stance all but silenced O'Brien. He read the two failed resolutions in court and made two points: "The board is unanimous in declaring its support for the valuable and important function which the High School League serves, and the second point, and the point I would like to conclude with, is that the split on the Hopkins School Board with respect to the rule points up as well as anything I can think of the difficult decision which the Court faces."[9]

In contrast, Donohue questioned the value of litigating the case at all. "We are concerned when there is so little wrong which causes such great litigation," he said. "We question, Your Honor, the seriousness of her claim and the seriousness of this particular issue being in this court at this time."

Before the trial began, Judge Lord himself had joked about the case, laughing about the prospect of girls wanting to wrestle with boys. Why should the court system be involved in such a silly issue? Later, Wexler would recall a brief exchange with the judge in his chambers, where he had gone to have Lord sign a court document: "As I was walking out, he called after me, he said, 'Wexler, do you really think this is a serious matter?' And I said, 'You know, Judge, when I first started working on it, I didn't think it was serious. But I do now.'"

Reading the transcript decades after the events, I found myself reacting with anger and confusion. Witnesses diminished the practice and skill of these two high school girls, offering generalizations about all girls' athletic performance and hypothetically ranking them against random male competitors. The rule in question had been established to protect a class system designed to offer girls more athletic opportunities in high school, yet it was being used to shut two girls out. Peggy and Toni were painted as demanding girls unwilling to accept their schools' timetables for girls' sports teams. Plans were in the works. Committees had met. Girls' interscholastic teams were coming. Tech and Eisenhower would certainly launch girls' teams— eventually. Why should Peggy and Toni embarrass themselves by competing against boys, only to ruin the future of girls' athletics?

But they lacked the luxury of time. High school was coming to a close. For decades, male students had been offered a broad menu of interscholastic athletic teams: they could choose from interscholastic football, soccer, cross-country running, skiing, curling, basketball, wrestling, swimming, gymnastics, track, baseball, golf, and tennis. Peggy and Toni would have a chance to compete only if a federal court judge allowed them to play on existing boys' teams.

By 5 p.m. on Wednesday, April 26, Judge Lord thanked the attorneys and adjourned to write his decision. "You have really moved with alacrity," he said. "I think we have all of the essentials here in terms of evidentiary material and arguments, and I will do my best to try and give you my advice at an early time."

"Girl Athlete Injuries Called Problem," read one newspaper headline covering the final day in court. The story closed with a comment from LeVander: "The issue is not one of discrimination based on sex, he said, because the physical differences between the sexes amply justify the rule. 'Women start out with a basic physiological handicap,' he said."[10]

7

DECISION

At 8:40 a.m., Monday, May 1, 1972, Judge Miles Lord was ready to cut to the chase. He had finished hearing the last of both sides' testimony just four days earlier; now, he'd invited the four attorneys for a morning conference in his chambers. The discussion began with a review of two recent decisions from Nebraska and Michigan courts.

The Nebraska case involved Debbie Reed, a Norfolk High School student. She wanted to play on the boys' golf team, but the Nebraska School Activities Association forbade it: "Girls and boys may not compete on the same athletic team, and girls and boys may not compete against each other." There was no girls' golf team. On April 12, 1972, Judge Warren Urban of the U.S. District Court, District of Nebraska, issued a preliminary injunction in favor of Reed, permitting her to play with the boys' team until further order of the court.[1]

In Michigan, Cynthia Morris and her doubles partner, Emily Barrett, wanted to play on the varsity boys' tennis team at their Ann Arbor high school. The Ann Arbor School Board agreed to support the girls playing on the boys' team despite a prohibition within the rules of the Michigan High School Athletic Association (MHSAA). Unfortunately, the girls' opposition preferred to claim a forfeit rather than play against the doubles combo. On April 27, 1972, the day after Judge Lord adjourned in Minnesota, federal court judge Damon Keith issued a preliminary injunction invalidating the MHSAA rule and enjoining the association from "preventing or obstructing in any way the individual plaintiffs or any other girls in the State of Michigan from participating fully in varsity interscholastic athletics and athletic contests because of their sex."[2] Judge Keith stated that denying the girls the right to play high school sports on account of their gender violated their right to equal protection under the Fourteenth Amendment.[3] Morris would later attend Carleton College in Northfield, Minnesota, where she played on the women's tennis team and was Peggy's nemesis on the court during their college careers.

Judge Lord said that he thought that when the Minnesota State High School League became aware of these two cases, which had just been decided in the past few days, it would probably agree to allow Peggy and Toni to play on their teams pending their appeals. Bernhard LeVander quickly noted that he had reviewed the cases, but the league was not changing its position. Instead, he emphasized a decision involving the Louisiana State High School Athletic Association in which the court ruled that a student's athletic eligibility did not rise to "federal proportions."[4] "We are talking about the question of whether or not, because we have a couple of exceptional girls who are exceptions to their class—the class of girls—that we are going to strike down the entire bulwark . . . [T]hese girls aren't being discriminated against in any sense that they are being treated differently at that school than other girls," LeVander said. "All the girls at St. Cloud are treated the same and all the boys are treated the same." It was "preposterous," he claimed, for a student to presume that they had a "right to insist that a school is going to provide them with a chance to go out for a sport." He continued: "It isn't even a question of denying a youngster an education; it is not a question of denying or withholding a chance for them to go to school. We are talking about a chance to play in an athletic contest. It just seems to me that it is way outside the bounds of what the federal courts should be concerned about and should be involved in, in trying to determine whether an individual should play or shouldn't play on a team in a school."

Judge Lord countered immediately: "If it is so unimportant for this girl to participate, why is it so all-fired important that the League resist it with such fervor? Why don't they just let her play, if it is not an important thing?"

Donohue replied that schools were already attempting to "remedy the wrong." Why should the courts and taxpayer dollars be involved just to appease a student who doesn't think the district is moving fast enough? At this point, however, Judge Lord put a stop to the debate and explained that his opinion was complete—and it was adverse to the league: "I have drawn an order directing that the girls be certified as qualified to compete by the high schools, and the order also enjoins the League from taking any sanctions against the high schools or any other teams against whom these girls might compete, and it is effective immediately." He added, "I am only ruling on these two girls in this circumstance."

Lord raised one other point with the attorneys during the conference, saying he felt he owed it to all of them to explain his active role in the proceedings. He felt that the ACLU should have had more legal experience when it took on this case and shouldn't have given the case to Wexler to handle by himself. "When I first met with Mr. Wexler . . . I suggested that on a case of this dimension, he get some help," he said, recalling the discussion at a pretrial conference in his chambers. "I didn't know the dimension of the case, but it looked to me like a substantial and complicated case and the ACLU assigned one young lawyer . . . I am not sure what the Court's rule is: maybe somebody will advise me. But when a young lawyer comes in faced with three lawyers of some experience and his first case in a situation like this, I thought . . . it called for some judicial intervention to even the scales."

At this point, LeVander was none too happy about having to show up in Lord's chambers to learn he had lost the case. "I would like to add an objection now to the conduct of the Court in the course of the trial . . . in intervening in the case, in trying a big part of the case on behalf of the plaintiffs," he said. "I just think that ought to be on the record . . ."

The content of the court's decision is not hard to read or understand, although the MSHSL would later complain that it lacked clarity because one exception to its rule could certainly lead to more. In the decision, issued May 1, 1972, the U.S. District Court for the District of Minnesota held that Peggy Brenden and Toni St. Pierre had shown that they "could compete effectively" on the boys' teams they sought to join (tennis, cross-country running, cross-country skiing) and that there were no alternative competitive programs sponsored by their schools. Thus, a rule prohibiting the girls from participating in boys' interscholastic athletic programs was "arbitrary and unreasonable, in violation of the equal protection clause of the Fourteenth Amendment" and application of the rule could not stand.[5] The attorneys for the schools and the MSHSL had contended that sports participation was a privilege and not a right that needed to be protected by the Constitution. The court stated that it had jurisdiction in the matter because although the MSHSL is a voluntary organization, it was authorized by Minnesota statutes and relied on member school districts in decision-making and rule enforcement, which meant it was "acting under color of state law."[6] The MSHSL, with its governmental support and powers, was misusing its authority by excluding girls from sports teams.

The court rejected the notion that Peggy and Toni had failed to seek "administrative remedies" rather than rely on the legal system: "Counsel have failed to establish that there is any viable administrative remedy which the plaintiffs could have followed prior to the commencement of this action." School authorities had been well aware of the girls' situations, and "there was obviously no program equivalent to the boys' programs in tennis, cross-country, and cross-country skiing." In addition, any review process would have returned to the girls' basic ineligibility due to the MSHSL rules forbidding them to compete on the boys' teams. And as recently as March 1972, the league's representative assembly had rejected an amendment that might have allowed such competition. "Where the administrative remedies are plainly inadequate, or where resort to those procedures would be futile, there can be no requirement of exhaustion of remedies," the court stated.[7]

In response to the MSHSL's argument that the court's decision would affect "all public high school students in the state in similar situations and all school districts in the state," the response was that this case did not demand that the court rule on the constitutionality of the rule in question. In fact, the court was careful to keep the boundaries of its decision quite narrow, noting that a basic principle of constitutional law is that the courts shouldn't formulate a rule of constitutional law broader than what is required by the precise facts, and constitutional issues shouldn't be decided in a case if there aren't facts to necessitate that. The decision goes on to carefully list the points it does *not* address: (1) "This Court does not decide whether participation in interscholastic athletics is of such importance as to be fundamental in nature." (2) "This Court is not deciding whether sex, as a classifying act, is suspect." (3) "This case does not involve a class action. It involves only the assertion of a violation of constitutional rights as to two high school girls." (4) "This Court is not deciding whether the league rules providing that there shall be no participation by girls in boys' interscholastic athletic events is unconstitutional or constitutional."

> What the Court is concerned with in this case is the application of League rules preventing participation of two female high school students in three sports at two high schools, involving two school districts. In addition, the factual situation is further narrowed because of the high level of competitive skill which these girls have achieved in their respective sports. An additional factor limiting the Court's decision is the absence of interscholastic competition in the relevant sports at the high schools attended by Peggy Brenden and Toni St. Pierre.[8]

The court pointed to the principles set forth by the Supreme Court in *Reed v. Reed*: a classification "must be reasonable, not arbitrary, and must rest upon some ground of difference having a fair and substantial relation to the object of the legislation, so that all persons similarly circumstanced shall be treated alike." Though there may be substantial physiological differences between males and females, those differences had "little relevance" to Toni's and Peggy's situations. There was no evidence that they, or any other girls or boys, would be in any way damaged by their competing in boys' interscholastic athletics. The girls had reached a high level of competitive achievement in their sports and should not be denied access to the boys' teams because of their sex.[9]

The presumption that the girls' participation would "hamper the development of other girls' athletic programs" was a "vague and undocumented fear," the court stated. "Peggy Brenden and Toni St. Pierre should not be sacrificed upon this altar." Although the league would rather avoid challenges to what it felt to be a "highly desirable rule," the court pointed out that prohibiting Peggy and Toni from competing with boys became "unreasonable in light of the objective which the rule seeks to promote." In this factual circumstance, applying the rule to them was "arbitrary and unreasonable, in violation of the equal protection clause of the fourteenth amendment."[10]

The court ordered:

1. That Peggy Brenden and Toni St. Pierre be declared eligible to compete on their respective teams at their respective high schools.
2. The Minnesota State High School League is enjoined from imposing any sanctions upon either St. Cloud Technical High School or Hopkins Eisenhower High School for compliance with the Court order, and that no sanctions are to be imposed on any other public high schools for engaging in interscholastic competition with St. Cloud Technical High School and Hopkins Eisenhower High School.

8

VIOLATION OF THE FOURTEENTH AMENDMENT

Within days of hearing the court's decision, the Minnesota State High School League's directors gathered in a special meeting to review the outcome and determine the organization's next steps. Rather than focusing on compliance, they voted unanimously to appeal Judge Lord's ruling, an action they announced the same day Peggy played her first tennis match for the Tech team. The MSHSL wanted the Eighth Circuit to reverse the lower court's decision, stating the appeal was intended "to fulfill a commitment made in 1969 to develop an interscholastic program for girls."[1]

"Our idea is to establish separate programs for girls and boys, without a cross-over," Dorothy McIntyre said. "Our girls' program is designed to give equitable competition; so a girl has a chance, and can receive a feeling of success."[2] The MSHSL took the federal court decision as a direct affront. It did not like to be questioned about its authority and rules, and allowing two girls to play on high school teams populated by boys was not at all what it wanted. Announcing an appeal within days of the decision was one way to show how strongly the league felt. It would wait for the appeals process rather than take any action that would open up additional boys' teams to girls. No new girls' state tournaments were scheduled for 1972–73.

Marvin Helling, associate executive director of the MSHSL, shrilly warned about Minnesota's experience at a national conference hosted by the American Association for Health, Physical Education, and Recreation (AAHPER). Helling was a former Minnesota high school teacher and coach who had had a celebrated ten-year run as head football coach at the University of North Dakota. He claimed the addition of girls to boys' teams would have a "devastating effect on the competitive opportunities available to girls." He also contended the courts were responding to "special interest groups in hot pursuit of their selfish goals; over-zealous parents seeking an additional gift for an already gifted daughter; a talented girl using the free legal counsel available for the fun of it (it's exciting, and puts down the establishment); the girl who would rather win one more medal, one more ribbon or one more match, rather than win the big one which would be a victory for all of the girls who want a program." Helling closed with an exhortation that likened the court's decision to a sexual assault.[3]

News of the decision elicited a mixture of messages. Peggy received a few notes from family members and friends, saying, "Right on!"; "Congratulations on the stand you took, the battle, and the victory"; and "Happy to hear your 'physiological differences' were not so great after all." One of our aunts wasn't so sure the victory was all that big a win: "It didn't sound as if much got changed but just for you two girls. I suppose you were working for more of a deal than that."[4]

"Nothing from our position has been solved," said Michael Donohue, the St. Cloud School District attorney. "Miss Brenden and Miss St. Pierre are the only winners, though the MCLU is probably happy with the ruling too."[5] An editorial published in the St. Cloud Tech student newspaper argued that the decision creates "inexcusable confusion," opening the doors for more costly legal suits: "The school stands on shaky ground of not knowing if it will be involved in the next lawsuit designed to test the rule."[6] A *Minneapolis Star* editorial saw it differently:

> The legal victory won by Peggy Brenden of St. Cloud Tech and Antoinette St. Pierre of Hopkins Eisenhower High School is part of a growing body of case law that does advance women's liberation. So the case is a breakthrough.
>
> Both girls—young women is perhaps the right way to put it—are fully capable of competing with their male counterparts. Lord's rationale thus boils down to the view that to

deprive Ms. Brenden of the chance to play tennis, or Ms. St. Pierre to run and ski in state league events, was arbitrary, unreasonable and denial of equal protection of the law.

This does not, however, automatically destroy sports programs, of which there are really very few for female high school pupils. Nor does it mean that the Minnesota State High School League must automatically open the door to all comers. Nevertheless, there probably will be other individual challenges.

This case is important on several levels, not just as it affects sports. Still, both the women's liberation and the legalistic viewpoint can, it seems to us, be reduced to this common sense point: These young women are able to compete with male opponents out of school, so why not for their school?[7]

Despite the dire possibilities outlined by witnesses in court about what could accompany mixing girls and boys in competition, no one seemed to think it would be all that difficult to implement the actual decision. St. Cloud Tech principal Charles Sell said, "Miss Brenden will be allowed to compete as dictated by the court. Whatever ability she has will be able to come forth at that time." The school's athletic director didn't anticipate any problems, either, since the decision involved just one Tech girl. "I've always felt that if girls as a whole group were allowed to compete with boys, it would hurt the teams," George Potter said. "This involves just the one girl here."[8] Coach Bill Ritchie doubted competing against boys would be all that great for Peggy. He said that she would start at midseason ranked last on the team and would have to work her way up.[9] "She is ranked among the top in the nation among women, but even some of our boys who are not ranked highly can beat her," he told the student newspaper.[10]

Eisenhower's athletic director, George Reynolds, was unconcerned about implementing the court's decision. He said of Toni, "She has been working out with both teams and has been with them practically all the time. I haven't heard anyone speak out against it. By girls' standards, she's pretty good. Whether she'll be able to make any one of these teams remains to be seen, though."[11] It wouldn't be until the following school year that Toni sought a spot on the boys' teams, but much would happen in the coming months.

In Hopkins, the school board composition changed almost immediately after the decision. By the end of May, two new women had been voted onto the previously all-male board. The board's position on Toni's case and its support for girls' athletics had been the subject of much local news coverage; it is not clear whether that was the reason for the change in the gender balance. The Hopkins newspaper called newly elected board members "two hard campaigning ladies whose only similarity seemed to be their femininity" and noted their edge over the male incumbents may have been that neither was employed, giving them more time for "campaigning and coffee partying."[12]

Rather than focusing on the MSHSL appeal, the Hopkins School Board took a different approach. By late June, the board committed to providing interscholastic girls' sports in each of the district's two high schools. Each school would have three teams, one for each season. There would be swimming and skiing, tennis and volleyball. Both schools would sponsor track-and-field teams in the spring.[13] The boys had thirteens sports to choose from, regardless of which school they attended. By comparison, St. Cloud Tech's student handbook for the 1972–73 school year listed eleven boys' interscholastic sports teams; some had already compiled a full schedule of competition, including the newest addition, hockey. But the handbook now mentioned six girls' interscholastic programs: tennis, golf, gymnastics, basketball, swimming, and volleyball.

As the school boards decided to give girls an opportunity long provided to boys, their actions were often portrayed as a move to steal boys' resources. A *Hopkins Sun* headline announced, "Girls' Sports Get Go-Ahead; Boys' Athletics Take Lumps."[14] The Tech student newspaper proclaimed, "Girls and Hockey Bust Budget," explaining the new boys' hockey team would receive $12,000 and girls interscholastic athletics would get $7,000—"enough to support seven sports."[15] Ironically, both the St. Cloud and Hopkins school districts had just opened new high schools in 1970 and, without hesitation, had added a large menu of boys' sports to each of them. Though the schools in each city were less than four miles apart, they would not be sharing coaches, facilities, or teams. But this expense had not been singled out as a budget-busting move. Without debate, the community had subscribed to the belief that boys on both sides of town deserved equal access to athletic opportunities. That was only fair.

In contrast, the decision in Peggy and Toni's case, which pushed two schools to provide two girls with athletic opportunities equal to those of boys, was highly controversial. And the MSHSL would not let it go uncontested.

9

PEGGY'S MATCH

Peggy learned of her court victory by reading the local newspaper. On Monday, May 1, 1972, the front-page headline read, "Court Rules City Girl May Compete with Boys."[1] That was really all Peggy needed to know. Perhaps our parents were given more details interpreting the case and its ramifications. But high school students were largely left out of the loop. Judge Lord's decision was never announced at a team meeting; none of Peggy's teammates cheered or congratulated her; and our family had no celebratory dinner. "I don't recall any great celebrations about any aspect of winning," Peggy said, "whether it was the lawsuit or a tennis match. It was not something we spent a lot of time reliving."

Most of the Tech players seemed to be unaware of the court proceedings required for Peggy to play a tennis match with them. Her teammates neither rallied around her nor shunned her. While she had been practicing with them for weeks, they had only a vague idea of what was going on. Jeff Peterson, a junior who played both singles and sometimes doubles on the varsity team, would recount later, "It wasn't that much on my radar. I was aware of it in the background. My sister was in the same class as Peg, so she might have told me."

Grant Helgeson, a sophomore and the No. 1 singles player on the team, said simply, "I had no idea—no idea." In fact, decades later he said he did not know about the federal court case involving his teammate. Grant's younger brother, Kent, who also played tennis that spring, said he really didn't give much thought to what it took for Peggy to play on the team. He was attending South Junior High at the time. "I'm just an eighth grader," he said. "I was just glad *I* was playing on the team." It was rather remarkable that Kent had gained a spot on the varsity tennis team. Jerry Sales, who created St. Cloud's junior high team and coached the junior varsity players, admitted later that he wasn't entirely sure whether it was legal to play a junior high student in high school matches. But no one ever challenged it. The St. Cloud coaches just felt lucky to have the talented Helgeson family in their school district.

The Helgesons—Grant, Kent, Brace, and later their young sister, Ginger—were raised to play tennis. They had every opportunity to develop their game: ample coaching, court time, and encouragement. In the winter, Grant and Kent would hit indoors at racket clubs in the cities and at St. John's University. Their father, Jerry, had been a star athlete at Tech, claiming the state championship in discus in 1950 and 1951. He had also been an All-American cocaptain of the University of Minnesota football team. Jerry and his brother Don owned the family business, first called Jack Frost Farm and then Gold'n Plump Poultry, which began as a hatchery business and evolved into a major broiler production and marketing operation.[2]

Grant used the phrase "spoiled little country-club kid" to sum up his teenage self. "I'm the oldest. I'm Jerry Helgeson's son. I'm No. 1 on the tennis team, captain of the football team, father is the largest employer in St. Cloud, member of the country club. We've got a tennis court in the front yard, and we've got a racquetball court in the basement," he recalled. With his blond locks, blue eyes, and influential family, Grant epitomized the fair-haired boy. A summer driver would take him and his brother to tennis tournaments, traveling to cities like Duluth and Brainerd. "We played tennis every summer, all day long," Grant said. Both he and Kent recalled their dad giving them the choice to do family chores or practice hitting tennis balls against the wall in their racquetball court. "He used to say, 'It's thirty minutes downstairs or chores. You decide,'" Kent said. "Easy choice." Building racket skills was part of their daily routine. Grant even half-jokingly commented that he thought his parents divorced over their own mixed-doubles competition. Tennis was central to the Helgeson family identity.

During the previous winter, Peggy, along with both Grant and

Kent, had participated in a special program to promote junior tennis. They were among twenty select players (four girls and sixteen boys) from around the state who received both coaching and competition offered on Sunday evenings from October 1971 to February 1972.[3] They often traveled together to the indoor tennis clubs in the Twin Cities area, a valuable opportunity because of both the quality of the coaching and the access to indoor courts, which didn't exist in St. Cloud. Grant credits Peggy with saving his life because of the "transportation support" she provided, certain her driving skills kept him and Kent safe on what otherwise might have been some very risky trips. He points out that as a sixteen-year-old, he had seven accidents in his first year of driving. "And they were all my fault," he added.

No one on the team seemed to have anything against Peggy's participation. In fact, Bill Ritchie told one newspaper that the rest of the team was on Peggy's side.[4] "I thought Peg handled herself with complete grace. She was just a terrific competitor and absolutely positive on the court," said Jeff Peterson, who competed for the same spot in the lineup as Peggy. "All of us immature boys would have little tantrums out there. People would throw rackets and all sorts of stuff. She never did anything like that. I was always impressed with her demeanor on the court. I enjoyed having her on the team."

"I don't really want to say she was just one of the guys, but she was just one of the guys," Kent said. "She was just one of the tennis members on the team. We really didn't think of her as an alien, a girl on the team. We thought it was just great 'cause she strengthened our team." Peggy liked her teammates, too—they were "good guys." She felt comfortable teasing and laughing with them. She enjoyed riding to matches and swapping brownies, apples, and sandwiches from the bag lunches the school provided. And she liked hearing everyone's slightly embellished accounts of match highlights.

No one made a fuss about a girl participating. "That was the cool thing about all those guys on the team—it was just not a big deal," Kent said.

Yet for Peggy, it was a big deal—a very big deal. Her coaches and team didn't seem to acknowledge the unusual circumstances that placed her in their midst. They simply accepted that Peggy had been "forced" onto the team by the judge, Coach Ritchie said. "When the order came, the order came. I didn't have any choice. She was part of the team . . . I didn't make an issue out of it. They knew how good she was."

There wasn't any media speculation about how adding Peggy might strengthen the Tech varsity lineup. It was more about whether she would *be* in the varsity lineup at all. Peggy explained to reporters that she was starting at the bottom. "I'm No. 7 right now," she said.[5] "I hope to play No. 3 singles. I'll just have to compete for the spot."[6]

"I have a good tennis team," Coach Ritchie said. "She's going to have a tough time in the position she's in because she's going to have to beat a lot of good tennis players." As he saw it, even though it was midseason and she'd been practicing with the team, Peggy would start out at the bottom rung of the roster.[7] She had gained permission to play on the team, but now she must prove she could compete. She didn't get into the lineup immediately for the match against Elk River on May 2, but Coach Ritchie said she could play in the May 6 match in Coon Rapids. Jeff Peterson had a music contest preventing him from making the trip, so Peggy would fill in at the No. 3 position.[8]

That meant Peggy would need a team warm-up suit. She didn't go to the girls' gymnasium in Tech's basement to pick up the clothing. The girls' physical education department didn't have any tennis uniforms. Girls purchased their own (terribly ugly) blue snap-up jumpsuits for gym class, and the department provided tank suits (color-coded by size) for swimming instruction. Instead, the boys' athletic department issued Peggy's warm-up, which she carried home with the excitement of a treasured Christmas present. It wasn't until she got to her bedroom that she pulled out the bright orange fleece pants and sweatshirt, which were adorned with black and white stripes down the legs and around the cuffs and a tiger head on the back. She pulled on the pants and rolled up the waist to keep the hem from dragging on the ground. The fabric wasn't all that soft or fluffy; it was a heavier gauge of fleece intended to keep wet (male) swimmers comfortable when they stood on the pool deck. It had been shared by multiple students before Peggy and undoubtedly had been laundered many times before it landed in Peggy's hands—hardly a fashion statement. Yet the pilly warmup was a badge of team membership, proof she was part of the team. While her teammates had long ago become accustomed to representing their school in an official uniform, she had never had that experience. Suited up in that school-issued warm-up, Peggy felt the immensity of the court's decision. She was a St. Cloud Tech Tiger! She wore the outfit to bed that Friday night, and she would keep it on through her entire first match. "I thought that warm-up was the coolest thing," she said.

Our family drove to Peggy's first match on May 6. She, of course, traveled with the team, sitting in the front seat with Coach Ritchie. The players were all dressed for action. Coon Rapids, a suburb north of Minneapolis, was one of the metro-area schools Tech played each season. The team drove on Highway 10 west out of town, past the reformatory, and through an assortment of small towns: Clear Lake, Becker, and Big Lake.

Coach Ritchie wasn't particularly big on small talk, so the front-seat conversation was sparse. He may have been feeling annoyed, having been peppered with questions about Peggy in anticipation of her first official match. Up until now, none of the team's other matches had captured the attention of reporters. No one had asked about Tech's top two singles players, Grant Helgeson and Jeff Schwanberg, who were undefeated. The coach felt they were the ones who deserved coverage. Tech High School had a very good tennis team. It ranked among the top fifteen schools in the state,[9] and with more than half the season completed, the team was undefeated.

It was rather blustery when the Tigers finally walked out onto the Coon Rapids tennis courts. Spectators were waiting. Tennis typically didn't draw many fans; even parents didn't come to all their kids' matches, and there were no bleachers or chairs. Wearing jackets, hats, and even scarves, the spectators stood outside the chain-link fence in temperatures hovering around 50 degrees. Photographers from the *St. Paul Pioneer Press*, the *Minneapolis Tribune*, and the *Coon Rapids Herald* aimed cameras at the court. Sandy and Jim brought their Super 8 movie camera to capture snippets of the match, though it wasn't a good day for pictures: the courts were surrounded by a drab gray sky, a parking lot, and a fence that provided no protection against the 10-mile-per-hour winds. The fans stood by the fenders of boxy-looking cars or sat on curbs to watch. I felt tense and nervous as I moved in and out of our blue Chevy.

I had watched my sister play dozens and dozens of tennis matches—one of the fringe benefits, or burdens, of being the youngest sibling. I knew how to watch tennis, how to clap for winning shots and stay silent for errors. My mom sometimes couldn't help herself and let out a gasp or groan when my sister hit a net cord. I knew better. I watched Peggy play feeling both protective and proud. The other spectators didn't seem to share this sentiment.

As usual, Peggy was slightly queasy when she walked out on the court. This wasn't an unfamiliar feeling; she often began her matches with that churning in her belly. She used her warm-up time to help her relax, focusing on the basics—watching the ball, moving her feet, breathing deeply. Then she started to watch her opponent, sizing up his possible strengths and weaknesses. The insight she gleaned minutes before the match would be the only "scouting" reports she would have to guide her strategy.

Peggy was pitted against a Coon Rapids boy named Steve Krause. He was a senior with short brown hair, white shorts, and a T-shirt. Mostly he played in the No. 2 spot that season. At the start of the season, it looked as though he might challenge senior Dave Steelman for the No. 1 singles role on their team. But for this match, against St. Cloud Tech, against Peggy, Krause was placed in the No. 3 position.[10]

"Peggy Brenden won't affect how I play my team," Coon Rapids coach Bob Pivec had told a reporter days before the match when he had not yet decided who would play against her. He added, "When good men play good women players, they respect each other's ability."[11] For that May 6 match, Pivec opted to place one of his most experienced seniors in the No. 3 spot rather than asking one of the sophomores who usually played that position to endure such a high-pressure match. Coach Ritchie didn't realize at the time how the opposing team had adjusted its roster. "They stacked their lineup basically because the No. 3 didn't want to get beat by a girl," Ritchie said. "If I'd known that, I would have said something."

Stacking a lineup is frowned upon by high school tennis coaches because it makes the outcome of matches dependent on coaching decisions made off the court to create intentional mismatches. But the lineup change Peggy encountered was not done to help the opposing team win—it was done so that nervous male opponents were saved from match pressure, saved from playing under intense scrutiny, and saved from the prospect of teasing and taunting should they lose to a girl. The Coon Rapids sophomore who had been moved from No. 3 to No. 2 lost to Tech's Jeff Schwanberg 6–0, 6–0.

In her match, Peggy used what she called "meat and potato" tennis. She chose smart, high-percentage shots, nothing fancy. She reminded herself that she didn't need to press to win every point. She could allow her opponent to lose points, too. She gave herself silent pep talks: "Krause is nervous, too." "Let go of mistakes." Peggy felt like she was playing for girls everywhere; it was a level of pressure she had never encountered. "I really wanted to win that one," she said.

Throughout the court case, the Minnesota State High School League had worked to portray Peggy as a generic representative of her gender and her individual characteristics and talents as immaterial. And now, in this very first match, Peggy felt as though she carried the weight of her entire gender. It wasn't Brenden v. Krause but Girl v. Boy.

Dressed in her full warm-up with a white collared shirt and her hair in a ponytail, Peggy split-stepped and then sidestepped efficiently from ball to ball. Her shots were often lofted high to force her opponent deep. Both players came to the net, sometimes because they forced each other there by hitting short balls. Peggy moved Krause back and forth and up and back on the gray-blue court. They fought doggedly, separated by the three-foot net.

Behind the chain-link fence at one end of the tennis court, Peggy could hear a man heckling. He chided her for being there, telling her she didn't belong on the court and shouldn't be playing against boys. No one intervened, and she never mentioned it to either coach or to her teammates. Peggy concentrated on staying under control, physically and mentally. She tuned out the voice and focused on the match. She knew seeing an opponent get angry or show frustration lifted her own game and was always careful not to give that edge to anyone else. Years of playing along alleyways and public parks had taught her not to allow distractions to become an excuse for losing.

The play went on and on, the pressure building. Peggy's teammates finished before her and sat on the nearby courts, watching. The match was a test for both players, a long, nerve-wracking battle. She stuck with her usual mental game: "Kill 'em with cool." Head up. Work yourself out of this. Never show a sign that you're struggling. Peggy's expression remained serious but impassive.

Both sets went beyond the usual six games. I grew sweaty and uncomfortable, waiting for the match to end. I sat silently, rooting for my sister, but I could not will her to victory. Krause claimed the final win, 9–7, 7–5.[12]

Krause didn't toss his racket or flaunt his victory but simply went to the net and shook Peggy's hand. She described him as a very nice kid. (I will note that my sister has never bad-mouthed her opponents, even the ones who irritated her and attempted to psych her out. Krause did not resort to any questionable tactics or gamesmanship.) Being a good sport mattered to Peggy, and she made a point to be gracious in both victory and defeat. She respected that trait in others, too.

Krause confessed to a reporter that "his legs were so wobbly he had trouble standing."[13] "I really hope she keeps playing," he said. "She earned the right. I'll root for her."

For Peggy, the loss was a discouraging blow, and the drive home felt much longer than 60 miles. She wished she had gone to the net more often. She wished she had been more consistent. She hated losing. The loss was painful and frustrating. Even the orange-and-black fleece warm-up failed to offer comfort in the face of a stinging disappointment.

This had been Peggy's first chance to play tennis as part of a team. Up until now, she had only experienced the game as an individual, rising and falling on her own performance. Being part of a team adds another dimension to the game, creating motivation to play for your team's success, not just your own. Players get to celebrate a team win, even when losing their own match. Yet Tech's team success didn't seem to translate the same way when it came to Peggy.

As a team, the St. Cloud Tigers had decisively beat Coon Rapids. Yet reporters all led their stories with the pronouncement of Peggy's loss. "Peggy Bows in Debut; 'I Choked,' She Says" was the headline of a *St. Paul Pioneer Press* story. The story began, "Peggy Brenden played her first game of tennis as a member of the St. Cloud Tech team Saturday and lost. The 18-year-old senior who was allowed to compete in interscholastic boys competition was the only member of her team, in fact, who didn't win as the Tigers defeated Coon Rapids, 4–1."[14] The *Minneapolis Tribune* headline was "Girl Prep Enters Boys' Area, Loses."

Coach Ritchie found the media coverage quite annoying. "[We] beat them 4–1 and the article in the paper was all Peggy. I didn't appreciate that," he said. "I'm sure the boys resented it because the focus wasn't on Tech winning or what Tech was doing; the focus was on Peggy playing." Peggy heard the coach's disappointment. He told her he was surprised her summer tournament experience hadn't better prepared her for the match pressure.

Now that the legal maneuvers were over, Peggy's story shifted from the local news section to the sports pages, but I don't think the sportswriters were accustomed to dealing with high school girls. Their intent seemed to be to treat her as just another athlete, yet they couldn't help singling her out. One article made a point to explain where and when Peggy dressed and showered after the match and that she had a babysitting job afterward.[15] Another noted her height and weight, something I've never seen referenced in a story about other high school tennis players.[16]

She was No. 3 in the team lineup again for Tech's next match against Elk River. Peggy split sets with her opponent, Bob Elveru, who had played No. 1 singles ten days earlier against Grant Helgeson when Tech had played Elk River at home.[17] After a long battle, Peggy lost in three sets: 4–6, 6–2, 4–6. She said Elveru didn't seem like a seasoned tennis player, but he played with a fierce intensity, as though losing the match would mean "losing face." Once he even frantically climbed up the chain-link fence, reaching to retrieve one of Peggy's shots. The Tigers again claimed the team victory 4–1.

Every match was important to Peggy, but she could see that her opponents played as though defeat might be a fate worse than death. Coaches were finding that the possibility of losing to a girl rattled their players and altered their lineup. The tennis coach at Brainerd High School, Bud Schmid, told a reporter, "The question is, 'Who goes against Peggy?' Nobody wants to for the fear of getting beat."[18] For these high school boys, losing to a girl carried a stigma. It was worse than losing to your little brother or your grandpa, and it was far worse than losing to your most hated rival. It was the most humiliating of losses. In the macho world of male athletics, losing to a girl unleashed ridicule, even from your friends and teammates. The opposing players clearly felt it was a "big deal" to play against Peggy, Kent Helgeson said. Coaches had to find a player who was willing to take the risk of losing and capable of enduring the taunts that would inevitably accompany even a well-played defeat.

"It was in the 1970s—there is very much a 'boys vs. girls' thinking," Peterson said. Some people tried to make girls feel guilty about the loss of status boys endured when defeated by a female competitor. Peggy never bought into that notion.

On May 15, Tech took on Apollo at the newer high school's state-of-the-art courts on the north side of town. Only two years earlier, Apollo's coach, Mac Doane, had led the Tech team, and some of his current Apollo players had previously played for Tech. Steve Helgeson, a senior, didn't feel a strong sense of rivalry. Tech's players were former teammates, friends, and in the case of two boys, family: he and his brother Scott Helgeson, a sophomore who often played No. 1 singles for the Apollo team, were cousins of Grant and Kent. Like their southside family members, they had grown up playing family tennis, attending summer tennis camps, and competing on the junior high team. They also had a tennis court in their yard; hitting balls was always on their "chores" list, too.

At this intercity match, Peggy captured her first win of the season.[19] Playing No. 3 singles, she beat Steve Helgeson (6–3, 6–3), who recognized Peggy but did not really understand the circumstances that had placed her as the only girl in the school match. "I really did not know that she had won a court case," he said. Having played tennis with girls often at camp, he didn't find it all that strange to compete against her. The last time Apollo and Tech faced off, he had been assigned the No. 2 singles position, where he had bested Jeff Peterson 4–6, 6–4, 6–4.[20] Tech had won that earlier match 3–2, but this time the team blanked Apollo, 5–0.

Though all of his teammates had lost their matches, too, Helgeson immediately heard teasing about his defeat. "I just sort of shrugged it off," he said. "And then Mac Doane, the coach, said the same thing and made fun of the fact that I had lost to a girl." Doane, who was a friend of the Helgeson family and a local legend, didn't compliment the strength of his player's opponent or talk about how he could have adjusted his game. He instead offered up an insult to embarrass his captain and, at the same time, unthinkingly disparaged Peggy, whom he had helped introduce to the sport.

Helgeson, stinging from the dig, brooded about it all night. "The next day, I didn't tell anybody," he said. "I just walked into Mac Doane's classroom and I said, 'I quit. I'm not going to be your captain when those kinds of things are said.'" He did not return to compete again.

Peggy would go on to make two more trips with the boys' team, winning matches in straight sets in Brainerd and Litchfield. The Brainerd coach said his player was so upset by the loss that he vowed he would never play a girl again.[21] News coverage of Peggy's wins was brief—no extra attention for victories. But she was proud to see notches in the win column. Still, Coach Ritchie was only willing to have Peggy play singles. He felt that she didn't hit with enough "authority" to be a doubles player. He knew she was consistent, but he thought doubles required more power. He never attempted to find her a doubles partner or mix her into the doubles lineup. "I knew that she was upset with me when I didn't let her play doubles," Ritchie said. "She wanted to, and she asked me, and I told her no."

Unlike many high school tennis players, Peggy was an experienced doubles player, having competed in doubles as well as singles draws during summer tournaments. Ritchie later expressed regret for his decision: "I think if I had more maturity, I would have worked her into doubles because she was consistent, and that also wins in doubles."

As the playoffs approached for the Minnesota high school boys state tennis tournament, Ritchie had to narrow his lineup. In the single-class system the MSHSL used at the time, only one doubles team and two singles players could compete for each school. In order to select the two singles players and two doubles players to enter in the district tournament, Ritchie set up a singles playoff between Peggy and Jeff Peterson. That challenge match would determine who would be in the lineup for the second singles spot.

Winners at the district tournament moved on to the regional, which is where they could capture a state tournament berth. Given the Tigers' 12–1 dual meet record, there was a good chance the team would advance. Jeff, who played both singles and doubles, had a 4–3 record in singles. Officially, Peggy's record was 3–2 for her more abbreviated season. She did have three exhibition wins as well, against two girls and a boy from Moorhead High School. But those matches didn't seem to matter in determining Peggy's place in the lineup. (I suspect that if she had lost them, they would have had more of an impact.) Peggy's record also didn't take into account the lineup shifts made by the opposition—as Grant noted, once Peggy started playing official team matches, the competition changed. "It was pretty well known that whoever Peggy played was going to be their best player," Grant said.

While tennis offers a clear method for ranking players, a ladder built on head-to-head competition, coaches know there is more to consider than ladder play to determine the composition of their teams. For example, a top doubles team often pairs one of the team's best players with a player who brings the best chemistry or complementary style of play. In singles, Ritchie noted that although Jeff Schwanberg could sometimes beat Grant Helgeson, Grant had more success playing in the No. 1 position. Hence, after a couple of matches, Grant played No. 1 most of the season. Excellent doubles players who understand court coverage and strategy may not rise to the top in head-to-head singles competition, but coaches watch to see how they perform in matches and experiment with pairings to find the best mix. "The doubles is definitely subjective," Ritchie said.

But in Peggy's case, it all came down to head-to-head competition. Ritchie asked her and Jeff to play one six-game set at the junior high school. Jeff, a tall, slender boy with floppy blond hair and black rectangular glasses, figured the coach chose the location, which was a few blocks away from the usual high school practice courts, to minimize curious spectators. Peggy and Jeff had played off more than once during the season, but this time, the outcome would determine who continued into postseason play. A lot was riding on very few games; in tennis, momentum can easily shift between sets, but here they would be playing just one.

Both players felt the pressure. Both wanted to claim their place on the roster. But it wasn't personal, and there was no antipathy between the teammates. Jeff did recognize that Peggy's win could mean that she might be the first girl to ever play in a Minnesota state tennis tournament and that, as a senior, this was her only opportunity. "It meant something," he said.

They both played hard, but Jeff pulled out the needed six games. "It was very close," he said. "I won 6–4, and Peg was very gracious." Peggy headed home, and Jeff returned to school, not feeling exactly celebratory about his victory. "I remember going back to the locker room and realizing that everyone seemed to know we were playing this challenge match," he explained. He was surprised to discover that what had seemed to be an individual competition was the subject of locker-room buzz—boys who played baseball or ran track were wondering what happened. The very first person Jeff encountered, who was not even someone on the tennis team, asked about the outcome. "I told him, and a cheer erupted. It felt very wrong," Peterson said.

The Tech Tigers went on to capture the District 19 tennis title. Coach Ritchie slotted Kent Helgeson, the eighth grader who had played doubles throughout the season, into a singles position. Grant Helgeson and Jeff Schwanberg, who had paired together for their first doubles title at the end of May during the White Bear Lake Tennis Invitational, represented Tech as a doubles combo at districts and won the District 19 doubles title.[22] The Helgeson/Schwanberg team was very successful, going on to win the regional tournament and reaching the finals of the state tournament that year. In an epic two-hour, fifteen-minute final match, they finally fell to Edina's Chris Barden and Dixon Dahlberg 6–3, 3–6, 10–8, taking second place in doubles and giving the Tech team second place in overall competition. It had been twenty-five years since Tech had sent a team of any kind to a state tournament, and this was the school's first state tournament finish in its tennis history. Edina, a longtime Minnesota tennis powerhouse, claimed the championship, earning the most points in singles, doubles, and team competition.[23]

"When we went to state, [Peggy] wasn't in my state lineup," Ritchie said. "Coaches said to me, 'We wouldn't have played her,' and I said, 'You wouldn't have had a choice.'" He added, "Looking back, I wish I would have put her on the tournament team where coaches *had* to deal with us."

When I interviewed Coach Ritchie, more than forty years after Peggy's case, he repeated over and over that I should tell Peggy he was sorry. He was sorry that he had just started his tennis coaching career when my sister showed up, asking to play on his team. He was sorry that he was not yet confident or experienced enough in his role to dare to partner her with a teammate for doubles or include her in his state tournament lineup. "She didn't make my state tournament team," said Ritchie. "If I had more experience, she would have. I feel bad that it was too early for Peggy and me." Ritchie, a large, soft-spoken man, also served as a deacon for his church. His thirty-one-year tennis career at Tech included three state team championships, nine runner-up finishes, five third-place finishes, and an 84 percent winning rate. He was inducted into the Minnesota Boys' Tennis Coaches Association Hall of Fame in 2004.[24]

As a green coach and teacher, Ritchie received no counsel from school district administrators or the athletic director about how to handle the groundbreaking court case and new team member. Neither did he hold any team meetings or communicate with his players about Peggy's presence. Though everyone knew it was unusual to have a girl in their midst, no one ever talked about her court challenge or how to incorporate her into the team. "I didn't resent it," Ritchie said. "I hope I didn't send that message. But I probably did . . . I don't know what she went through, to be honest with you. I'm not happy with what I did, looking back on it."

There was no tennis banquet or awards ceremony. Peggy remembers simply being summoned to the athletic director's office before the school year finished. Mr. Potter opened a drawer and handed her a fuzzy orange T. His only comments for the occasion were "Here it is." In Peggy's opinion, earning a letter was about the most prestigious thing a high school student could do. She had watched pep rallies where the band played and students applauded and whistled while athletes collected their badges of accomplishment. She very much wanted to claim one herself.

Though she received the first varsity letter Tech High School ever awarded to a girl, it happened privately, without fanfare, a handshake, or even a word of acknowledgment. It was handed over briskly between a change of classes. Letter jackets did not even exist in girl's sizes, and Peggy would never wear that letter on her sleeve. This particular letter would be seen only by friends and family who asked to page through her scrapbook. "I'm sure no one else knew I got it, but that was OK," she said. "I knew it."

10

TONI'S RACE

Toni was likely running on the cinder track near Eisenhower High School when she heard about the court's decision. She was part of the Eisenhower girls' track team that practiced at nearby Maetzold Field, named for Russell "Butsie" Maetzold, a teacher and much-heralded Hopkins coach.

The team had started in spring 1971 with a small group of girls, one coach, and a big box of gold cotton T-shirts. Leaping over hurdles, handing off batons, and tossing shot puts was brand-new to most of the girls, and likely they weren't in peak condition when the season began since they had no experience with training or preseason workouts. Toni, who loved long distances, competed in shorter races of a half mile or less. Longer distances weren't an option for the girls. Because this was an extramural team, the schedule would be limited to three meets.

In 1972, Eisenhower decided to field an interscholastic girls' track team. Only a few girls would have known about the opportunity—the Minnesota State High School League didn't list the state meet on its official calendar of events until March 1972. The calendar, published at the start of the school year, was important to all the public schools in the state because it contained the dates for statewide drama and music festivals, district and regional tournaments, alternative dates for some contests, and all the boys' state tournaments. The MSHSL didn't mail information about policies and qualifications for the May 27 state girls' track meet to athletic directors until mid-March; the boys' track teams typically started practice by the beginning of that month.

The longest event in the girls' 1972 state meet would be an 880-yard run, two laps around the track. Though a longer distance would have played more to Toni's strengths, she still chose to be part of the girls' track team. In the courtroom, MSHSL officials had warned that gifted girls opting for boys' teams would gut the future of girls' programs, leaving the girls' teams with fewer athletes. But Toni never really considered participating on the boys' track team. This would be the first year any girl could compete in an interscholastic state tournament, and she was excited to have that chance. She was an experienced runner at this point, and her race card for the upcoming summer included the National Junior Olympic track meet at the Air Force Academy in Colorado Springs and the state and national AAU championships in Burnsville, Minnesota, and Canton, Ohio.

But for many of the 458 high school girls who earned the chance to compete in that first state track meet, it was a big stage that felt strange. Most had only recently been introduced to their events and had had very limited opportunities to test their skills in formal competition. As the first Minnesota Girls State Track Meet approached, many had competed only a handful of times. In order to be eligible to participate in the MSHSL state meet, the league only required a team to participate in two other track meets, which is a brief schedule by any measure.

And this interscholastic sport wasn't just unfamiliar ground for the girls—Hopkins coach Paul Bengtson freely admitted he wasn't really a "track man." Yet he didn't let that stop him from becoming Eisenhower's first girls' track coach. He asked the Hopkins athletic director for the job. He believed girls should have athletic opportunities, and he had previously started girls' track, gymnastics, and bowling activities at Mound High School, in a smaller Minnesota school district, where he had been athletic director. They weren't full-fledged interscholastic sports, but the girls had coaching and a smattering of competition. Bengtson, who was also an assistant football coach and head wrestling coach with three state titles, had a teenage daughter, and he believed that sports participation could be every bit as beneficial for high school girls as it was for boys. So he offered to single-handedly coach the girls' track team. The two women who

taught physical education with him at Eisenhower were not convinced that offering interscholastic athletics was a good idea; they
came and observed a few practices but did not take part in any coaching roles. Bengtson relied on the advice of the boys' swim coach to
help him train Toni, the strongest runner on the team. He knew she
was his most experienced and skilled athlete and gave considerable
thought to her training as he devised a demanding regimen modeled
after the workouts the swim coach used.

The boys' track coaches kept their distance, neither helping nor
interfering. That suited Bengtson just fine. He acknowledged he
knew nothing about high jump and only a little about weight events
such as discus and shot put. He focused on running.

On Saturday, May 27, 1972, the day of the MSHSL State Girls
Track and Field Meet at St. Cloud Apollo, Toni stepped up to the
starting line, ready for the gun. Wearing a loose-fitting team T-shirt
and her wavy dark hair pulled into pigtails, she ran neck and neck
with her competitors for part of the race until she used a powerful
kick and broke away. One racer from Sibley High School in Mendota
Heights was expected to be a strong contender, but she stumbled and
fell, twice, though she still got up and finished. She was quite coura-
geous, Bengtson said.

"Toni St. Pierre of Eisenhower thrilled the crowd with a record clocking in the 880-yard run. She completed the race in a national record-breaking clip of 2:18.3. The old mark was 2:18.8," the
St. Cloud Daily Times reported.[1] The *Minneapolis Tribune*'s high
school sportswriter, Bruce Brothers, who rarely covered girls, chose
to share one highlight from the MSHSL's first girls' statewide event.
At the bottom of his column, he included a brief paragraph men-
tioning Ruth Harris, "sister of Sibley miler Tim Harris. Tim has the
best high school times in the mile this year." Brothers didn't offer
Ruth's times or any information about her performances other than
highlighting her speedy high school brother. The account of the
880-yard race also mentioned that Toni had passed Ruth and that
the latter had stumbled and "nearly blacked out 40 yards from the
finish line."[2] No mention of Toni's national record. This brief bit of
coverage seemed to reinforce an argument often used to keep girls

and women out of athletics: they just weren't up to such rigorous physical activity.[3]

Athletes like Kathrine Switzer had heard a similar refrain: women lacked the endurance and stamina necessary to run long distances. Rather than letting women attempt to train and compete, officials simply barred them from entering races at all. Still, Switzer decided to register for the Boston Marathon in 1967 despite the absence of a women's division. She used only her initials and obtained race number 261. "Two miles into the 1967 Boston Marathon, an official tried to eject me from the race simply because I was a woman," she said. "The marathon was a man's race in those days; women were considered too fragile to run it. But I had trained hard and was confident of my strength. Still, it took a body block from my boyfriend to knock the official off the course and allow me to complete the 26 miles 385 yards."[4] Switzer's audacity to claim a spot in the race resulted in her suspension from the Amateur Athletic Union; she said the reasons given for the suspension were (1) running with men; (2) running more than 1.5 miles, which was further than women were allowed to go; and (3) running without a chaperone.[5] Women were supposed to follow many rules, and the consequences for breaking them could be swift and harsh.

It would be five years later, in April 1972, just before Minnesota's statewide girls track meet, when the Boston Marathon recognized its first official female champion. Women were demanding the chance to put on an official number and compete, even when the races were long and demanding.

Just as Minnesota's high school girls were getting their first chance at a statewide track-and-field meet, the MSHSL was excitedly celebrating the fiftieth year of the boys' event, which would draw a crowd of five thousand spectators. The official program highlighted the golden history of the meet, with Sig Ode, the Minnesota State Department of Education official who had testified in court, writing the content. It was a "labor of love," according to Ode. "A tribute to the sport of the gods." He wrote, "The annual state track and field meet permits the largest array of athletes in Minnesota to demonstrate their athletic prowess to a single audience on a single day . . . by passion, sacrifice, and the will to dare greatly, they contributed to the human spirit."[6] It would be a day of heroics—male heroics.

There was a different tone to the media coverage of the girls' state track meet. It was light, highlighting things such as the crowd's colorful clothing.[7] One reporter pointed out that the winner of both the 100- and 220-yard dash, Jane Oas, found four-leaf clovers before each of her qualifying races. No mention that Oas, a Mound senior, would be competing in the 1972 Olympic Trials in July. The reporter did ask the winner of the softball throw whether she aspired to play for the Minnesota Twins.[8] (Ha, ha—no!) The *Minneapolis Tribune* placed its story next to a local feature about the trolley by Lake Harriet in Minneapolis opening for the season. Perhaps editors didn't view the girls' state track meet as a historic athletic event, or maybe the 16–2 drubbing Texas delivered to the Twins was the sports-page priority that day.

An article from the previous year highlighting the strong interest statewide in girls' track had likewise landed in the *Minneapolis Star*'s Variety section, not the Sports section. Under the headline "Girls Getting Pretty Darn Good in Track," the article noted that Moorhead, Minnesota, coach Paula Bauck appreciated the help of her husband and son, who each drove a car full of her tracksters to the meet because the district's support for the team didn't include any expenses such as transportation.[9]

Girls received a mixed message about their participation in sport. Schools offered a few athletic opportunities but were quick to note that girls did not participate in the same numbers as boys, so it wasn't worth the same investment. Girls depended on the boys' teams to share their equipment and facilities, because those things seemed to belong to the boys, not the girls. There were unwritten guidelines that seemed to govern how girls should behave as athletes. According to Connie Sugden, the White Bear Lake girls' track coach whose team shared first place with International Falls at that first 1972 track meet, "We try to keep the girls as feminine as possible, and just let them run."[10] Sweat, muscles, aggression, self-confidence, and toughness were not usually included in anyone's definition of "feminine." Girls who embraced those characteristics risked the scorn of their peers, their parents, and their communities. It was as though "female ath-lete" were an oxymoron. Yet girls flocked to the newly created teams.

Though his girls' team was new and coaching track was some-what unfamiliar, managing dozens of novice athletes did not con-found Coach Bengtson. He thought it was fun and rewarding, and he was upbeat with his team. But somehow his role as Toni's coach seemed to place him at odds with the MSHSL and assorted oth-ers. Bengtson was the subject of a "strong letter of censure," a rather rare public scolding issued by the MSHSL to coaches for failing to abide by league rules. The violation: allowing two junior high girls to run in a track meet—more specifically, as published in the *MSHSL Bulletin,* a violation of Article 1, Section 9-B-I of the Athletic Rules for Girls, page 94. When the letter arrived, Bengtson was shocked. The infraction had occurred when his team was competing in a dual meet against Richfield and he wanted to add two eighth-grade girls into the lineup so other girls wouldn't need to run three or more events. He called the opposing coach beforehand and asked whether she would mind. "I thought the more girls running, the better," he explained. The Richfield coach didn't object, but the MSHSL did. "I was really upset about that censure," Bengtson said. "I wasn't try-ing to break any rules." The censure's impact was largely symbolic, without any real consequences except to irritate Bengtson, who cared deeply about his reputation as a coach.

MSHSL girls' rules differed from the boys' in many ways. The age limitation was just one. Eighth-grade boys could compete on the team of a high school that was "continuous" with their educational path; seventh and eighth-grade girls were not eligible at all. Mutual agreement between coaches did not create an exception to eligibility rules, according to the league handbook.

Toni did not find her way into running until after eighth grade, when she was drawn into the running world by a timed race in her gym class. Many classmates dreaded the standardized tests used in their physical education classes: sit-ups, standing broad jump, 50-yard dash, 600-yard dash, and more. But for Toni, the class footrace was motivating. As the date of the race approached, she prepared. "I was belligerent enough," Toni said, "that I wanted to be the fastest runner in the school. I stopped smoking for a week before the race so I could run that race fast."[11]

Patrick Lanin, who was Toni's science teacher at Hopkins West Junior High (grades seven through nine), heard about her speed. Lanin contends she set a school record and ran away from the competition. He sought Toni out and told her, "I think you could be a good runner if you set your mind to it." And he offered his help: "You can come out and run with the boys if you want to." At first, Toni didn't respond with enthusiasm, giving him a "whatever" sort of reaction that junior high school teachers must endure all too frequently. But he had planted an idea, which may have arrived at just the right time. Toni had developed a reputation for behavior issues in the classroom, Lanin said. She was distrustful and rebellious. "She had a little bit of a wild streak to her," her brother said. Running would be just the thing to channel her energy and time into something constructive.

When Toni was twelve, her parents split up. Toni, Sam, and their mother left Staples, Minnesota, and moved in with grandparents Mitzie and Oscar Loosen, sharing the couple's white three-bedroom rambler, which they modified to create an extra bedroom in the basement to accommodate the sudden influx of family. The house sat atop a hill overlooking Minnetonka's Shady Oak Lake with plenty of outdoor space to run. Grandma Mitzie, an opinionated Austrian German, initially forbade Toni from running competitively. She told her granddaughter it wasn't good for girls—it wasn't ladylike. But Toni was the type of kid who kept running because she was told she shouldn't. Though from different generations, both grandmother and granddaughter were strong-willed. On this matter, Toni would triumph, and Grandma Mitzie would eventually become her devoted fan.

Likely Mitzie, a devout Catholic, influenced the decision to send Toni to a Catholic girls' school in the fall of 1970. Toni started her sophomore year at St. Margaret's Academy, not the Hopkins public high school where Lanin had recently started coaching the boys' cross-country running team. There was no girls' cross-country team at St. Margaret's, so Toni followed some of Lanin's workout schedules as his Eisenhower team, a powerhouse, posted a 15–0 season.

She also participated in AAU events. Late in the fall, St. Margaret's did send a group of girls to the AAU National Cross-Country Meet in St. Louis, Missouri. Riding in an old converted hearse, which leaked carbon monoxide through the floor, several of the athletes became sick. Though they were able to compete, they performed poorly. In the middle of that school year, Toni transferred to Hopkins Eisenhower.[12]

Lanin believes it was an all-comers event at the University of Minnesota that really stirred Toni's competitive juices and fed her passion for running. She raced against women from the U's running club and won. He remembers exclaiming, "Do you realize what you did?" Passing college-age competitors stoked the teenager's interest.

Toni was drawn into cross-country skiing her junior year, undoubtedly influenced by her boyfriend, who won the individual state title in 1970 and 1971. Toni and her brother were already downhill skiers, learning at nearby Lone Lake ski hill, which had a rope tow powered by a gas engine. But it wasn't until December 1971 that Toni strapped on her first pair of cross-country skis. She practiced in the winter of 1972 with the Eisenhower team, which included many of the distance runners with whom she already worked out. With a golf course right outside the school's back door, the team had easy access to trails, which the team members maintained for daily training.

The 1970 opening of a second Hopkins school, Lindbergh High School, created a need for more coaches. (There was no debate about whether the new high school could afford to field a full complement of boys' sports; neither was there any discussion about finding coaches for girls' teams.) Lanin, a novice skier, was assured he had all the skills he needed to step in as Eisenhower cross-country skiing coach—it was simply cross-country running on skis. He knew about endurance training, and he knew how to build team culture. Plus, he could count on the assistance of a recent graduate, Tim Heisel, to teach technique.

Toni put in the miles and developed quickly, qualifying for the National Junior Nordic Championships at the Middlebury College Snow Bowl in Vermont that spring. She was showing promise, but she didn't try to inflate her standing in the courtroom. She testified that she could probably outski one or two boys on the Eisenhower team. But she knew she was improving quickly.

When Judge Lord finally issued his decision, it seemed to signal a whole new world for Toni's senior year: She could be part of two teams. She could run *with* her teammates and *against* strong competition. She was giddy, flying on cloud nine.[13] Unfortunately for Toni, however, she was not done running the gauntlet of obstacles that so often befell female athletes. Even though the league had lost in court, it would find its own ways to win, Heisel said.

Before school even started, Murrae Freng alerted Toni to a rule change he thought might impact her. It is hard to know how many students the MSHSL executive director personally warned of possible rule infractions, but somehow Toni came to mind. Called the Independent Team Play Rule, it previously applied only to three team sports—football, basketball, and hockey—but it had now been expanded to include more sports. Freng explained that it was intended to open up opportunities for more students to compete in organized sports as well as keep athletes from overextending themselves and committing to too many events and too much training. Though it officially was aimed only at boys, Freng said that because Toni would be competing against boys, it applied to her as well.[14]

The Independent Team Play Rule was changed in the MSHSL's 1972–73 Handbook after the Representative Assembly Meeting in March 1972. The league had called it to coaches' attention in August so that high school athletes who participated on interscholastic teams would not participate in independently organized meets or tournaments during or after the season in the same athletic activity. For Toni, that meant she could not run in both school and AAU events. She had to choose.

The new rule did have exceptions. It didn't apply to baseball or skiing, and plenty of boys would find their way around it by competing in distances different from the ones they ran in school. But the penalty for violating the rule was severe: the offending athlete forfeited all remaining eligibility in all athletic activities for "his" senior year.[15] Toni could lose her chance to compete in skiing with the boys' team and running on the girls' track team. So, although Toni was pictured in her high school yearbook seated in the second-floor window of an old farmhouse along with Lanin and the other cross-country runners, somehow the MSHSL had taken her out of the picture. She was hurt and angry; it was enough to make a runner, even a tough one, cry. It was also unnerving. Toni felt as though she was in MSHSL crosshairs. Her competitive opportunities were in jeopardy. She worried she might be one rule change away from getting side-lined again. "I have this dream that something will happen just before the season starts," she said.[16]

Toni was pushed off the team and pulled out of competition, and no one offered to throw a body block to keep her in the race. R. Michael Wetherbee of the Minnesota ACLU said he didn't think the MSHSL had the right to control students' activities with the Independent Team Rule. But Toni could see nothing was going to happen quickly enough to make a difference that fall.[17] Her decision was obvious. She was already washing dishes twice a week at a nursing home and working overnight shifts as a nurse's aide on Fridays and Saturdays to earn money to travel to the National AAU meet scheduled in Long Beach, California.[18] She had a history of competition in AAU, which had been exciting and encouraging. The same could not be said for her competitive experience in high school. She chose running in AAU events. "I guess I kind of figured that AAU is too big a thing to pass up," Toni said.[19]

She kept working out with the high school team and ran as an exhibition runner in some meets. Lanin, who did not see the logic in blocking Toni from competition, continued to coach her along with the boys. Unfortunately, the league frowned on this as well, and before the end of September, Lanin told Toni it was unfair to give her this special privilege. She had to stop running in high school meets altogether.[20]

The Eisenhower cross-country running team struggled with injuries that fall. Two top runners couldn't compete, and a third ran in spite of a chronic injury. "We were at about half strength," Lanin said. "We never had a lot of depth." Eisenhower did beat five of the state's top ten teams during the season, but it didn't advance to the state tournament.[21] Meanwhile, Toni was celebrated by her classmates not for her outstanding efforts as a runner or for her gutsy challenge to MSHSL rules but because she had been voted homecoming queen. She marched at the front of the Eisenhower High School Homecoming "People Parade" with a police car leading the way and the Ike's Army cheer squad behind her.

Toni kept her sights set on finding athletic opportunities to compete against other girls. In the fall of 1972, she won the hilly 1.5-mile Swain Invitational in Duluth in 8:36, one of the biggest meets in the state. (The event, which had more than seven hundred participants and a challenging course, was so renowned that the winner of the boys' division from 1972 was pictured in *Sports Illustrated*.) Toni also took first place in a women's 1-mile race at Theodore Wirth Park and a 2-mile AAU race at the University of Minnesota golf course. But while winning is nice, she wasn't just looking for races she could win—she wanted competitors who would push her to stretch her performance.

Finally, when snow arrived and Minnesota's cross-country ski season launched, Toni was able to compete with the high school boys' team. In the first meet, on January 8, 1973, she tackled the 5-kilometer race at Theodore Wirth Golf Course. The track was fast, the temperature was just barely above zero, and the wind was blowing 6–8 miles per hour. She placed fifth among the nineteen skiers, and Eisenhower beat Edina East handily. Toni continued to race at Lake Conference meets on January 16, January 23, January 29, and February 1 in conditions ranging from wet, slow trails with lots of water to fresh snow that became both icy and fast. She raced against eleven different schools, finishing as high as fourth against a field of thirty-one competitors. She was 2:30 behind the fastest skier and nearly 12 minutes ahead of the slowest.

As the season progressed, the cross-country team's top finishers were usually junior Don Lee and senior Mark Saufferer. But Toni's name did come up in sports coverage by the *Hopkins Sun*: "Toni (not to be confused with Anthony) St. Pierre placed eighth among 32 cross-country skiers in the triangular with West and Jefferson," reporter John Sherman wrote. "Yes, Toni is a girl, but all bundled up she's just one of the skiers. She competes on an equal basis and is vital to the success of the team."[22] Still, Toni could see that her competitors didn't always respond the same way to her that they did to other skiers. As she slid silently through the frozen woods, puffs of icy breath in front of her, she would call out "Track, track!" as she approached another skier from behind, a signal to step out of the groomed trail and give up the right of way. She found her competitors were less likely to heed her voice than a male one, making it harder to maneuver past them.

At that time, Minnesota's cross-country skiers were part of a larger high school ski team that included jumping and slalom. They were coached by different people and scored as separate teams during competitions, but their combined performance determined their standings in overall competition. Hopkins cross-country skiers had placed first in every state meet since 1967, yet Hopkins had never won the overall skiing championship. Lanin's 1973 Eisenhower cross-country skiers finished the season with a 12–0 record. Though the team's chances of winning the state title were slim, it would be a favorite in the division.

Despite her strong performance during the season, as district and state tournament dates approached, Toni was no longer in the lineup. That wasn't because she couldn't keep up; Lanin estimated that in the Lake Conference, one of the toughest cross-country ski conferences in the state, her results put her among the top fifteen boys. In addition to her high school meets, she was sandwiching multiple AAU events into her calendar, and she had qualified for the U.S. Ski Association national B team—something that took priority over high school competition.

"Toni Travels with US Team," read the headline of a brief story in the February 15 *Hopkins Sun*. "Hopkins Eisenhower's athletic whiz left earlier this week for a two-week skiing tour with the United States National Team. As a senior this year at Eisenhower High, Toni competed against boys and more than held her own." Her ski tour would include stops in New York, Ohio, and Canada.[23] When her Eisenhower cross-country team took off for the state tournament trail in Cloquet, Minnesota, on February 17, Toni was not among the 117 official finishers. To her teammates, her absence made sense:

competing with the U.S. National Team was an amazing opportunity, akin to a farm team for the Olympics. Coach Lanin had encouraged her to make the trip. Given the uncertainties of actually getting to be among the four designated skiers for Hopkins Eisenhower in the district and state meets and the obstacles high school competition had already established, her teammates understood why she might opt to leave her high school team behind.

That decision meant Toni was not part of the back slapping and congratulations that followed when Don Lee finished first, winning the state championship with a margin of 42 seconds and almost single-handedly sealing the victory for the Hopkins Eisenhower cross-country ski team. Lee would return his senior year to repeat as the state cross-country ski champion and be offered a full-tuition scholarship to ski at Fort Lewis College in Durango, Colorado, giving him an opportunity to train with Olympic Nordic ski coach Adolph Kuss. After a year, however Lee chose to forgo that scholarship and leave college.

Toni also decided to cut her travels with the U.S. National Team short, Heisel said. Concerned that she couldn't keep up with schoolwork, travel, and ski, she returned home. According to Lanin, even though she had scored enough points in high school competition, she would not earn a letter in cross-country skiing because she hadn't completed the season.

A three-sport athlete, Toni would finish out her senior year running on the girls' track team, this time focusing on the mile, which was now available to high school girls. In an effort to gain some national competition, Lanin arranged Toni's entry and travel to the Drake Relays, one of the country's top outdoor track-and-field events, held in April in Des Moines, Iowa. With a crowd estimated at eighteen thousand, temperatures in the midsixties, sunny skies, and 15-mile-per-hour winds, Toni claimed third place with a time of 5:04 in the women's invitational 1-mile run. Lanin figured her time was the tenth fastest in the nation, and he was convinced that with the time she still had left to train, she could easily be running in the mid to low 4:50s by the upcoming Minnesota Girls' State Track Meet.

But things didn't quite work out that way.

Toni trained with her team, participating in the mile, the 880, and some relays. Using tactics he learned from the school swim coach, Bengtson pushed her at practice to run multiple timed splits, breaking the mile into one-lap segments that she repeated with minimal recovery time. The goal: a 5-minute mile. "I was hard on her," the coach said. "I pushed her a lot, and she got very tired because she ran those splits fast. She was hurting." Lanin did not like Bengtson's approach, calling the training strategy a "disaster." Heisel also believed the many abrupt stops and fast starts would lead to injury. While it might work well for swimmers, both Lanin and Heisel were convinced the approach was ill suited to runners.

Toni's performance at the regional competition in both the mile and the 880-yard run qualified her for the state meet on June 2 at Rosemount High School. "I entered her in the mile and the 880 run in the regions because I figured she could win them both, and she did," Bengtson said. "And that meant more points for our team. What I didn't realize is that if she qualified in both events, she was required to run in both of them at the state tournament." On the day of the race, Toni wasn't feeling well and wanted to run in only the mile. Bengtson said an MSHSL official insisted that if she scratched in one event, she must scratch in both. So, she ran in both races.

Unfortunately, she didn't have the spikes required by race officials. Coach Bengtson had gone to a local sporting-goods store to buy spikes suited to the track surface, but he didn't know the precise spike specifications, he said. The store owner advised him that he had just sold spikes to a boy competing in the upcoming state meet, so he bought the same type of shoes. When a race official saw the spikes, Toni learned she would be disqualified if she raced in them. Somehow, she managed to find another pair, which she laced on tearfully before her race. "All I know was she was running in a different pair of shoes," Bengtson said. Toni finished fourth in the 880-yard run. Her rival from the previous year, Ruth Harris, claimed the best time with a record 2:17.3. Toni outperformed the field in the mile with a 5:13.9 time, a full 8 seconds ahead of the next runner. But it wasn't the 5-minute mile she had been working toward.

A week later, Toni ran in the All-American High School Track and Field Championships in Des Moines, Iowa, finishing fourth with a 5:02.7 mile run. Then, with high school diploma in hand and plans to become a nurse, she continued to look for more competition. She organized the seventh annual Hopkins Raspberry Festival 5-mile road race and won the women's title.

Despite having won state championships in the 880-yard and 1-mile races, Toni never received any scholarship offers for cross-country running, skiing, or track. She wouldn't have expected to—girls didn't get athletic scholarships. That fall, she attended the College of St. Benedict, a small Catholic women's college in central Minnesota, which had no teams for any of her three sports. Even though she had won a federal court case that allowed her to compete in high school, Toni's collegiate horizon seemed devoid of athletic opportunities.

But options were opening up. In 1973, basketball, swimming, and volleyball would become the first varsity sports at St. Benedict, though the addition of cross-country running was still ten years away. Determined to pursue her passion, Toni negotiated her way onto the cross-country team at nearby St. John's University, the partner men's college. "Toni is a good runner and a wonderful person," said Jim Smith, the St. John's athletic director, at the time. "She will have to compete as an independent because under the rules of the conference . . . only those who are enrolled at the schools can compete on the teams." Still, he raised no objections to a woman competing against men. Toni was not brushed off or told to wait for a women's team to emerge.[24]

Toni was part of an exciting era full of growing athletic opportunities for girls and women, and it was easy to confuse that growth with equality. But anyone who cared to do a comparison could see that while girls had more athletic options than ever before, they still fell far short of "equal."

11

"THE COURTS FORCED THIS ON US"

Women are getting a raw deal!

A female who persists in her athletic interests, despite the handicaps and discouragements, is not likely to be congratulated on her sporting desire or grit. She is more apt to be subjected to social and psychological pressures, the effect of which is to cast doubt on her morals, sanity and womanhood.

—*Sports Illustrated,* May 28, 1973

Peggy and Toni's lawsuit had stirred the pot. Girls all over Minnesota now saw a path to participate on high school teams. Athletes from large and small towns across the state were asking to compete with boys, mostly because there were no girls' teams.

Some contacted the Minnesota Civil Liberties Union for help. The organization fielded requests from Jody Nolen, the Litchfield tennis player, and Margaret Phelps, a Bloomington swimmer, who both wanted to compete on their high school teams.[1] MCLU president Matthew Stark said that the Minnesota State High School League might face a class-action suit in state court if it did not remove the restrictions preventing girls from playing on boys' teams.[2] Two girls from rural Anoka, Christy and Marcy Riggs, sought permission directly from the MSHSL to swim on the boys' swimming team (denied).[3] And federal court judge Philip Neville in St. Paul issued a temporary order restraining the MSHSL from keeping a sixteen-year-old Edina girl, Ann Freeman, from skiing with her school's prep slalom team.[4]

In November 1972, the Litchfield school superintendent submitted an amendment to the MSHSL 1972–73 Representative Assembly
to delete language prohibiting girls from boys' teams, but the assembly voted to leave the rule in place. Official delegates included more
than fifty men serving schools from all over the state as superinten-
dents, athletic directors, school board members, and coaches, as well
as one woman—Willetta Brown, a coach and physical education
teacher representing the Women's Advisory Committee.[5]

The MSHSL was banking on the Court of Appeals to reverse
Judge Lord's decision. The league was firm that allowing girls, even a
handful, to compete with boys would only lead to problems—better
that the existing boys' teams were protected from change while girls
waited for their own athletic opportunities to emerge. But an appeal
before the U.S. Court of Appeals for the Eighth Circuit, a court that
encompasses Minnesota, North Dakota, South Dakota, Nebraska,
Iowa, Missouri, and Arkansas, would take time.

While Judge Lord had taken only a few days to make a decision,
the Eighth Circuit would not move so quickly. A three-judge panel
(Donald P. Lay, Gerald W. Heaney, and Roy L. Stephenson) would
hear oral arguments in January 1973, well after Peggy finished her
tennis season and in the middle of Toni's senior year. The panel
would review the league's and Thomas Wexler's briefs (fifty-nine and
thirty-eight pages, respectively). The judges would rely on only an
hour of oral arguments and the existing case record—transcripts, ex-
hibits, and papers filed with the trial court—to determine whether
the previous court decision contained errors of law. The process
would involve no new witnesses or additional experts. Besides the
MSHSL and MCLU briefs, the only additional information considered would be two amicus curiae briefs, one from the National
Federation of State High School Associations and another from the
Nebraska School Activities Association. They urged the court to set
aside the findings of the trial court.[6]

The Nebraska brief pointed out cases in New Jersey, Illinois, and
Indiana where courts had decided that there was a "rational basis"
for separating boys' and girls' athletic competition and that it was

not in violation of the Fourteenth Amendment to prohibit girls from participating in high school athletics with male students:

> The Courts should not, and cannot close its eyes to the actuality, that all high schools and state athletic associations, throughout the country that have incorporated a rule prohibiting girls from participating on boys' teams, will be effected, regardless of the decision, and regardless of whether or not they presently provide a separate athletic program for girls. A ruling allowing girls to participate on boy's teams will have an enormous impact upon the entire educational system, and the high school athletic program . . . To allow girls on a boy's team would require them to be under supervision of a male trainer, or require the school to hire additional personnel, a female trainer, for what may be, (only) a single girl.

Plus, the brief continued, girls' participation would "necessitate a chaperone" and separate "health facilities" (which seemed to be a term for a locker room or changing room), imposing an additional expense upon the school. "Allowing a girl to participate on a boys' team would throw out of kilter a system of high school athletics."[7]

Wexler traveled to St. Louis for his first-ever appearance before the U.S. Court of Appeals. He arrived at his hotel the day before he was scheduled to appear before the panel, where he would be given just 30 minutes during oral arguments. He knew he needed to be primed for this legal timed test. He stayed up all night, lying on his hotel bed, fully dressed, mentally preparing to explain the intricacies of this constitutional issue. He stared at the ceiling as he ran through all the persuasive insight he might provide. "These judges deal with these constitutional issues all the time. They knew the issues," he explained. Still, when they raised a question, he needed to be ready to address it. "I had the answers," he said. "It was good I stayed up."

It was a windy, freezing day in St. Louis when Wexler arrived for the 9 a.m. oral arguments. The judges had questions ready for the attorneys of both the appellants (MSHSL) and the appellees (Peggy and Toni). The attorneys listened for cues about what each question meant and whether they signaled the leanings of the justices.

Lay: Are all sex-based laws unconstitutional, such as the draft?

Heaney: Is it relevant that there are no athletic activity opportunities for girls?

Lay: Do you think that the schools will fail to meet their responsibilities to provide programs for everyone?

Stephenson: Is it discrimination, if there are no athletics at all for girls?

Heaney: Couldn't we avoid damaging the girls program if we limit our opinion to the facts of this case where no program is provided to girls at all?[8]

All of this court action was set against the backdrop of a recently passed federal civil rights law, Title IX, which took effect June 23, 1972. U.S. Representative Edith Green, an Oregon Democrat, had partnered with Representative Patsy Mink from Hawaii to author the bill, which prohibited sex discrimination in education. Their goal was equal treatment for women and men in education. Senator Birch Bayh of Indiana was the chief Senate sponsor.

Title IX was intended to change the established practice of preferring male applicants and limiting women's access to educational opportunities. Women were underrepresented in higher education; they typically had to have better grades and test scores than male applicants to gain admission to college, and Harvard, Yale, Cornell, and other schools maintained admissions quotas of two women for every three men. Upon answering questions about when they might marry or have children, qualified women were routinely turned away from graduate programs, medical school, and law school.[9] The 1972 law was enacted to prohibit sex discrimination in every educational program that received federal funding and end sex discrimination. It is brief and to the point: "No person in the United States shall, on the basis of sex, be excluded from participation in, be denied the benefits of, or be subjected to discrimination under any education program or activity receiving federal financial assistance."

At first, no one really knew what it looked like to comply with Title IX, which impacts multiple issues—admissions, scholarships, financial aid, equal employment opportunities for students and pro-fessors, and student rules. It applies to all educational institutions, both public and private, that receive federal funds, including thousands of local high schools, colleges, and universities. Schools failing to comply feared the prospect of losing federal funds or facing substantial damages and attorney fees from court cases.

Title IX does not specifically mention "athletics" or "sports," yet they became enduring hot-button issues, perhaps because athletic programs, divided by gender at most schools, offered so many glaring examples of bias. From coaches' salaries and travel budgets to gym sizes and scholarships, female athletes consistently got the short end of the stick.[10] At the University of Minnesota's Twin Cities campus, for example, the men's intercollegiate sports budget was $1.2 million in 1971–72, while women's athletics received $7,336. Coaches bought loaves of white bread and bologna for sandwiches to feed the women's teams on road trips. Graduate assistants volunteered their time, and women's teams played brief game schedules because they lacked funding. After Title IX was passed, the university's 1973–74 budget would hardly be described as equitable, with $27,000 allocated for women and $2.2 million for men. In 1974, University of Minnesota swimmer Terry Ganley, who would become the first woman to earn All-American honors in any sport, had no travel budget to pay for her trip to the women's national championship. She sold T-shirts in the lobby of the building where the men's swim team practiced—which housed a newer, larger pool than the one at the "ladies gymnasium."[11]

Enacting Title IX did not immediately rectify gender imbalance. Hardly! But it triggered an examination of gender inequality within sports. [12] A 1973 cover story in Sports Illustrated pointed out the huge disparities: "The funds, facilities, coaching, rewards and honors allowed women are grossly inferior to those granted men. In many places, absolutely no support is given to women's athletics, and females are barred by law, regulation, tradition or hostility of males from sharing athletic resources and pleasures."[13] Title IX would give federal agencies rulemaking authority to implement the law, but that would happen very slowly, as lawsuits and resistance stalled the process. Final regulations were not released until 1975, and the deadline for compliance in colleges and universities wasn't until 1978.[14] The

National Collegiate Athletic Association (NCAA), the governing agency for men's intercollegiate sports, launched the strongest opposition to Title IX. Walter Byers, the NCAA's executive director, claimed the law could cause irreparable damage to men's programs. The association financed a major lobbying effort to minimize the law's application.[15]

Title IX hadn't yet become a public law when Judge Lord heard Peggy and Toni's case. But when the Eighth Circuit–U.S. Court of Appeals began its review, the new law seemed very relevant. In fact, the Eighth Circuit would be the first court in the country to reference Title IX.[16]

On April 18, 1973, the Eighth Circuit upheld Judge Lord's decision. Lord had focused on the Fourteenth Amendment's Equal Protection Clause, but the appeals court also noted that Title IX sought to specifically protect women's access to educational opportunities. The Eighth Circuit said that interscholastic athletics were an important educational opportunity and declared, "Discrimination in high school athletics constitutes discrimination in education."[17] Thanks to the MSHSL's appeal, the Eighth Circuit issued a precedent-setting decision.

Other girls across the country had also challenged rules banning them from boys' teams, but most often their claims had been resolved informally or heard by lower courts or tribunals. Those challenges would not be looked to for precedent, established as authority for other courts, nor were they connected to a newly enacted federal law. For example, Abbe Seldin in New Jersey gained the chance to try out for the boys' tennis team in 1973 thanks to representation by Ruth Bader Ginsburg and the ACLU, but she was confronted by a cold coach and teammates who taunted and mistreated her. Her participation was short-lived, and her federal lawsuit was dropped,[18] which meant there was no higher court review or published decision.

Peggy and Toni's case went into the legal record. Justice Heaney, writing for the three-judge panel that reviewed the case, stated, "There is no longer any doubt that sex-based classifications are subject to scrutiny by the courts under the Equal Protection Clause and will be struck down when they provide dissimilar treatment for men and women who are similarly situated." He continued: Deciding whether participation in interscholastic sports was a privilege or a right was not the key question. The question was whether the two girls could be denied the benefits of activities that were provided by the state for male students. "Females, whatever their qualifications, have been barred from competition with males on the basis of an assumption about the qualifications of women as a class." Failing to provide the plaintiffs with an "individual determination of their own ability" to qualify for these teams violated the Equal Protection Clause. The contention that altering the rule would undermine girls' athletic programs was speculative and without merit. What was clear was that Peggy and Toni's schools had "failed to provide them with opportunities for interscholastic competition equal to those provided for males with similar athletic qualifications. Accordingly, they are entitled to relief."[19]

That appeallate court decision meant the MSHSL would have to rethink its rules. "The decision involves those two girls," Murrae Freng said, "but it obviously means we are going to have to redraft our rule to fit the decision. Otherwise, any girl in the same situation would have an excellent chance if she wanted to take the matter to court. But, as of today, it doesn't mean boys teams are open to girls on a wholesale basis." Freng said the league would study the decision, change its rules to comply, and submit the changes as quickly as possible by a mail vote to the representative assembly, the organization's legislative body.[20]

The league was worried that a change to its rules would cause some schools to forgo creating girls' teams: "We are concerned that because of the budget squeeze in many schools, a few might want to take an easy way out and just provide one program, open to both boys and girls at a time when we are trying to foster additional girls' programs," Freng said. "Our concern is for the whole girls' program, not just for one or two girls who really excel."[21] With forty-three yes and three no votes, the assembly passed an emergency amendment suspending rules banning coeducational participation in sports. The suspension would remain in place "until July 1, 1974, or until such time as a new rule has been prepared and adopted."[22] Orv Bies,

MSHSL information director, said, "We didn't have a choice. The courts forced this on us."[23]

Sportswriters were appalled. "Minnesota high school girls will be permitted to go out for boys football teams—or any other boys' team—after the State High School League officially dropped its rule banning such occurrences Friday," Bruce Brothers proclaimed in his lede on the front page of the Minneapolis Sports section.[24] Brothers warned that a "mediocre track man can now switch to the girls team if he so desires." He felt the MSHSL was "passing the buck" to school districts, which would be forced to make rules preventing such antics.[25] How "degrading" it could be to certain boys' sports to allow girls to compete, lamented John Sherman, a Hopkins sports reporter. "The new rules for competition constitute a farce," he complained. Entire boys' varsity teams could try out for the girls' team leading to the "total destruction" of girls' sports. "The open play system has too many loopholes. It discriminates against girls. And worst of all, it may ruin a number of promising girls' programs," he warned. Sherman did not name any specific schools where "promising girls' programs" might be subject to ruin.[26]

Contrary to pronouncements like these, girls' athletic programs rapidly expanded. From the 1971–72 school year to the 1972–73 school year, the number of schools with girls' athletic programs grew from 198 to 302. By the end of the 1976–77 year, Dorothy McIntyre had rolled out eleven different statewide tournaments for Minnesota girls. Nationally, the number of high school girls on sports teams grew from fewer than three hundred thousand in 1970 to over one million in four years. The feared exodus of boys attempting to shift from well-established, well-regarded, and well-funded programs to take over the girls' nearly nonexistent teams did not come to pass.[27] In December 1973, the *Minneapolis Tribune* published a lengthy story in its *Picture* magazine about the enthusiasm and growth surrounding girls' participation in sports. The amount of coverage was very unusual, with eleven large photographs of female athletes in action: playing tennis, diving in high school competition, officiating a volleyball match, and coaching college field hockey. The story noted that close to four hundred Minnesota schools now offered girls' athletic programs and more than sixty thousand girls were competing statewide. "Women's athletic programs are experiencing such an unprecedented and successful boom that cries of 'discrimination' are becoming antiquated," said Joe Soucheray, staff writer. "At Hopkins Eisenhower and throughout the conference, girls are treated as athletic equals with the boys," George Reynolds stated—a little confusing given that boys had thirteen sports and a budget of $160,000 while girls had six sports and a budget of $15,000. Athletic directors promised that budget parity would come once sports rosters included as many girls as boys. Title IX received no credit for this surge, and the article seemed to minimize the impact of Toni and Peggy's lawsuit by contending that relatively few girls had chosen to join boys' teams. Still, Dorothy McIntyre did acknowledge that her worries about the court's decision had been misplaced. "The League was against the Court's favorable ruling for only one reason. We thought it would damage our plan for girls' interscholastic athletics," said McIntyre. "But it hasn't." She added, "Girls are making up for about 40 years of lost opportunities."[28]

While schools built girls' athletic programs, girls also took advantage of the chance to play on boys' teams. Jody Nolen of Litchfield, Marnie Wheaton of Minnetonka, Ann Henricksson of Mahtomedi (the first girl to play in the Minnesota boys' state tennis tournament), Cathy Brennan of Minneapolis, and Karen Gibbs of Hopkins were just a few who joined boys' tennis teams. In 1973, sophomore Margaret Chutich, now a Minnesota Supreme Court justice, decided to play singles on the Anoka boys' tennis team. She earned the second singles spot, sandwiched between her brother at No. 1 and her then boyfriend at No. 3. The next year, when the MSHSL sponsored the first girls' state tennis tournament, Chutich joined Anoka's girls' team, and in 1975 she won the state tournament.[29]

Peggy and Toni's court challenge jump-started girls' high school athletics. Though the girls' teams were a long way from being equal, the impetus was in place to at least create girls' programs. There would still be more battles about funding and facilities. But no longer could girls be left entirely out of the game. It would take years for Title IX to gain clout. But the arrival of more and more experienced female athletes onto college campuses would help propel change. The combination of young women with an appetite for sport and a federal law intended to equalize opportunity would serve as a major force for change.

On September 20, 1973, Billie Jean King squared off against Bobby Riggs in the much-ballyhooed "Battle of the Sexes." The Houston Astrodome was packed with more than thirty thousand fans, then the largest crowd ever to watch a tennis match. In addition, more than fifty million Americans viewed it on television. King was carried into the arena like Cleopatra by a troop of muscular men; Riggs entered with a giant "Sugar Daddy" sucker and an entourage of "Bobby's bosom buddies," who pulled him on a rickshaw.[30] The atmosphere in the Astrodome was, in one sportswriter's words, "part circus and part Hollywood premiere, part television giveaway show, and all bad taste."[31] Still, this was an event not to be missed. Households all over the country held viewing parties to see this odd face-off, and every viewer chose their own protagonist—Billie Jean King, the woman who had demanded higher pay for female tennis players and won Wimbledon that summer, or Bobby Riggs, the fifty-five-year-old hustler and self-proclaimed male chauvinist pig. We all wanted to see King, at the top of the women's tennis world, trade shots with Riggs, a loudmouth well-past his tennis-playing prime. This pop culture moment was full of trash talk and hoopla. Riggs attempted to put King in her place, but King triumphed in straight sets: 6–4, 6–3, 6–3. The ending made women everywhere stand a little taller. The match "legitimized women's tennis," King wrote. "It was the culmination of an era, the noisy conclusion to the noisiest three years in the history of the women's game."[32]

It was the kind of victory that female athletes encountered over and over again in a game where they would be mocked and scorned. Even when they won, others would immediately point out how little it meant, or how many others could outplay them.

12

STAND UP

The Tech High School I attended as a ninth grader in 1973, after the Eighth Circuit decision, had a very different set of options than when my sister made her mark. I'd argue that it was different *because* she had made her mark. New girls' teams sprouted up with each season. By the time I was a senior, I could choose from interscholastic basketball, cross-country running, gymnastics, swimming, tennis, track, and volleyball. A softball team was introduced and was moving toward interscholastic status. I jumped in with both feet, trying the hurdles and long jump, sharpening my fielding skills in softball, and becoming a five-foot-four-inch captain of the girls' basketball team. I shot buckets in our driveway and daydreamed of sinking free throws for a state tournament berth.

All these athletic opportunities popped up quickly, and I ate them up. Other girls were more hesitant. Like me, most of my girlfriends had no previous athletic training or team experience. We hadn't been exposed to conditioning, game strategies, or skill building. And we'd had very little encouragement: classmates, coaches, and family members said they found it painful or humorous to watch us play. Sometimes our lack of experience was used as evidence that our gender wasn't meant to compete in sports. We had not been raised to have any confidence in our current physicals skills and our capacity to develop them. One of my tallest friends said she was born klutzy and couldn't play basketball even though she had never been on a team; another friend said that when she mentioned the idea of swimming competitively, her mother warned that her shoulders would become "too wide."

Boys' sports continued to flourish at Tech. A hockey team was added, and the boys' tennis team captured the state championship in 1976 with a lineup that included two Helgeson brothers, Kent and Brace. It was a big deal—I know because the team bus arrived in town escorted by screaming fire trucks.

It wasn't until my senior year that I dared to try out for the girls' tennis team. More than thirty girls participated. After watching my sister practice, compete, and fight to play, I worried that I couldn't measure up, and it was difficult for me to muster the nerve to claim a spot. Like many female athletes, I felt like an imposter. I was not an experienced player with a long record of success. Lots of people could beat me. I had come to believe that certain performance standards were required to claim a place on the tennis court, and I didn't want to embarrass myself. I saw how hard my sister worked, how much time she practiced, how many matches she played. And I knew how hard it was for her to prove she belonged despite all her efforts. Finally, I decided to put that measuring stick away. I didn't need to be better than my sister. I didn't need to be better than the boys. I didn't need to be the best player at Tech High School. The team existed so I could build my skills and participate in a game that I was growing to love.

I played first doubles that year. I learned how to compete in match competition in front of spectators (a few, anyway). I learned how to encourage my partner and refocus my game when we fell behind. I learned how to practice and have fun. And I learned that I was good at the game, and I could be better. My team did not advance to the state tournament, and I was not awarded an athletic scholarship. But I did earn a letter. As far as I was concerned, the 6-inch orange T meant that I was an accomplished athlete.

I kept playing the game, competing in college, in adult leagues, and with lots of friends for the next four decades. I have no intention of stopping. But access to high school sports did more than give me an enjoyable and healthy pastime. My experience in sports led to employment and leadership roles—officiating college intramural games, teaching and coaching basketball for Upward Bound students, organizing women's golf-league events, coaching school and youth teams, covering sports for a daily newspaper, and running a youth sports club. Sport is an industry, a career choice, and a field full of opportunities. It is a powerful economic, social, and political institution. "We have for the first time ever in our history, a critical mass of young girls playing sports," said Mary Jo Kane, whose academic research focuses on gender and sport. In comparison to fifty years ago, Kane unequivocally proclaims, "our cup runneth over."

Girls' interest in and appetite for athletics have swelled. In 2019, the U.S. women's national soccer team jersey sold out, "becoming the highest-selling soccer jersey of all time, men's or women's," according to a sports marketing expert. "No one knows how many jerseys Nike could have sold because either its mindset or its algorithm resulted in an underestimation of demand."[1]

The explosion in participation hasn't yet translated into a corresponding growth in media coverage, however. In fact, according to a longitudinal analysis, women's sports coverage declined from 2004 to 2014.[2] While 40 percent of all sports participants are female, women's sports receive only 4 percent of all sports media coverage, according to a 2014 documentary created by the Tucker Center for Research on Girls and Women in Sport. "If your basis of comparison is 'Where do women's sports stack up against men's sports?' I would say we are second-class citizens," Kane said.

A report issued in October 2021 on gender disparities between men's and women's NCAA championships echoed that point. It pointed out "stark differences in spending and staffing . . . leading to inequitable student-athlete experiences" and noted that the NCAA, which has resisted Title IX's application to itself, has failed to put in place systems to identify gender inequities across championships, allowing them to persist.[3]

Despite a tremendous groundswell in female sports participation, girls and women continue to be underrepresented in media coverage, coaching, sports governance, and sports-related employment. In fact, the Tucker Center found that only 41.8 percent of female athletes were coached by women and only 20 percent of college coaching positions were held by women. Only 21 percent of high school coaches in Minnesota were female in 2015.[4] "The ideals of meritocracy and fair play embedded in sport make it difficult for people to believe that it provides advantages for some groups over others, and yet negative evaluations of women's abilities in sport are implicit to an extent unrivaled in nearly every other social institution," wrote Janet S. Fink, a Tucker Center Affiliated Scholar and associate dean and professor of sport management at the University of Massachusetts Amherst.[5] Women are missing in leadership roles in organizations ranging from youth sports to Olympic Committees. They earn lower salaries and prize money than men. As participants, they command less media attention, and the attention they do receive tends to focus on their physical appearance rather than their athletic skills or abilities.[6] In addition, "girls of color continue to be underserved and overlooked," according to Billie Jean King, founder of the Women's Sports Foundation. African American female student athletes are underrepresented in many Division I sports like lacrosse and swimming as well as emerging sports like rowing and water polo. Only 2 percent of head coaches across all three NCAA divisions are Black women.[7] Litigation and laws have not leveled the playing fields yet. Most likely girls and women will continue to do it themselves, with their presence, passion, and persistence.

For Peggy, high school athletics left a lasting imprint, and her involvement in the lawsuit proved to be a defining moment. After high school, she attended Luther College, a small liberal arts college in Decorah, Iowa. There were no athletic scholarship offers—in fact, the governing body for women's college athletics at the time, the Association for Intercollegiate Athletics for Women (AIAW), prohibited women who received scholarships from participating in AIAW-sponsored competition. But Peggy happily competed on the women's tennis team at Luther, a school with about 2,200 students. The team, led by women coaches, took on much larger schools, such as the University of Iowa, the University of Minnesota, and the University of Wisconsin. Peggy played first singles and first doubles, winning multiple collegiate tournaments and advancing to national competition. During the summer, she worked as a tennis camp counselor.

The lawsuit would influence her career choice as she moved from the tennis court to the courtroom. She attended the University of

Minnesota Law School, working as a tennis pro and college coach along the way. She practiced law and was appointed a workers' compensation judge for the State of Minnesota.

"Being in a position to help grow opportunities for girls in athletics was a totally unexpected gift in my life," said Peggy, who continues to play tennis regularly. "I learned in a very personal way to be wary of what is popular, because popular and principled—especially in matters of civil rights—do not always go hand in hand." She added, "The people in power in 1972 said a girl on a boys' tennis team was ill advised. Authorities predicted I would get hurt. They argued the boys I played with and against would suffer psychological damage. They suggested my playing with the boys would hurt the growth of opportunities for other girls to participate in sports. While there is no doubt these perceptions enjoyed widespread popularity in 1972, they were wrong."

Peggy and Toni, forever linked by legal precedent, did not cross paths again. In a state where people frequently have "small world" moments, somehow their lives and networks did not intersect.

Toni remained an endurance athlete her entire life. Her other passion was nursing, and she loved her work as an obstetric nurse. She was an innovator who cared for and supported pregnant women and new mothers struggling with addiction. Toni, who battled addiction herself, sought to create healthy outcomes for infants and mothers. She was known to share her weekends looking after babies, providing respite care for tired moms who lacked a support network. As a volunteer, she traveled to Nepal, Vietnam, and other developing countries to provide care for pregnant women.

In 2006, Hopkins High School inducted Toni into its Athletic Hall of Fame. Intensely disciplined and competitive, she used her experience as a distance runner and skier to train for marathons and triathlons. She was at the starting line for the inaugural YWCA Minneapolis Women's Triathlon in 2008 and soon began winning her age group and competing in national events. She participated in the YWCA's free clinics, sharing training tips and helping others improve. Toni set her sights on the Boston Marathon but was sidelined with a pain in her leg, which was later diagnosed as cancer of the smooth muscle. In February 2013, she died of cancer at age fifty-eight, only days before she was set to be honored with a special merit award on Minnesota Girls and Women in Sports Day.

For all her own athletic accomplishments, Toni was proudest watching her daughters cross the finish line in school cross-country and track meets. It was not just the sight of her own children in competition but "seeing the hundreds of girls," Toni said. That is when she felt both the emotion and impact of her court case.[8]

Peggy and Toni were never part of protests, and they did not hear loud rallying cries of support during their fight. They pushed through on their own, banging tennis balls and logging distance in a world uncomfortable with their choices. They repeatedly heard about the problems their participation would cause and about their inability to compete. As teenage girls, they could see inequality and unfairness, while others simply claimed they were being demanding. They could see opportunities, while others saw budget and eligibility headaches. It took a very long time, and a shift in attitudes, before anyone saw the legacy they left behind.

Decades after the decision, Peggy finally read the full court transcript, catching up on the two days of testimony she had missed. It was then that she felt an angry sting. She heard the voices of people who championed girls' athletics targeting two teenage girls, and she winced. It hurt, she said, to see the way educators, coaches, and MCLU staff "belittled my passion, disparaged my motives and accused Toni and I of recklessly endangering the future of girls' athletics." Even after a federal court victory, the MSHSL chose to vilify them, never acknowledging its role in obstructing their high school sports experiences or those of other girls waiting in the wings.

In 1995, twenty-three years after Peggy graduated, she received a telephone call from Bruce Hentges, the athletic director at St. Cloud Tech. He invited her back to her old high school to speak at a pep rally. "I was not exactly enthused about the invitation, given my history at Tech, but he was very persuasive and very kind, and I agreed to come," she said. She took the day off and traveled to St. Cloud by herself for the event. When Peggy walked into the gym that February morning, it was filled with four hundred or five hundred students in the bleachers, equally divided between boys and girls. Hentges stepped up to the podium to introduce her and began by asking all the girls who were part of an athletic team at Tech to stand up. All but a handful of girls were on their feet. He then said, "You know, if I'd asked that question when Peg was a student here, she would have been the only girl standing." And with that, a gym full of teenage students rose to their feet and gave her a standing ovation.

Peggy loves to tell this story. Living through her senior year, challenging her high school and the Minnesota State High School League, was a lonely battle. Her cheering section was small. Her courtroom victory and tennis match wins never elicited fist pumping or applause. But my poker-faced sister confesses without hesitation that goosebumps ran down her spine as she heard the thunder in the Tech gym. It was a moment she never could have imagined.

ACKNOWLEDGMENTS

In 2005, I asked my sister Peggy whether I could write a book about her high school tennis experience. She gave me the green light. "It was exhausting enough to live it," she said. "I don't have the energy to write it." So I took up the cause, starting with a tape-recorded interview with her in September 2005.

Immediately, it became apparent to me that I couldn't write this book based only on my sister's high school memories and perspective. It had too many dimensions, too many players. I interviewed Thomas Wexler, the pro bono attorney who handled her case; he told me about Ruth Bader Ginsburg's assistance. Then I interviewed more family members. On March 8, 2006, I taped an interview with Judge Miles Lord. We sat around a large conference room table at his law office, where he worked after retiring from the federal court. He told me he had 96 percent name recognition in Minnesota upon leaving the bench and casually dropped the names of his friends Hubert Humphrey and Walter Mondale into our conversation. He said he had once hoped to write a book about *Brenden vs. Independent School District 742* because he was very proud of the decision. I could tell that in his version of the book, Judge Miles Lord would be the central character. I had something else in mind.

But my progress on the book stalled for more than a decade. Working as a research librarian in large, fast-paced law firms and raising three teenagers, I could not find the time for research and writing. By the time I picked up the baton again, Toni St. Pierre had died. I would never hear her account of the story. I began to work with more urgency, building a list of sources and reaching out to more and more people. They were all so gracious. Some came to my home; others met me in coffee shops. Priscilla Lord, Miles Lord's daughter, agreed to an interview during the pandemic, and we met outside in my front yard. Some people had astonishing recall, while others offered only snippets of memories. But nearly all spoke with fondness and admiration for Peggy and Toni, although very few knew much about the content or significance of their lawsuit.

My book does not document every interview or conversation with a note or citation. But I want to acknowledge the many people who gave me their time, answered my questions, and shared their recollections. A few are no longer alive, but they were all crucial to this story: Gary Anfenson, St. Cloud Tech tennis coach and chemistry teacher; Paul Donald Bengtson Sr., Toni's track coach; Constance Crane, Tech English teacher; Sue Fischer, St. Cloud tennis player; Timothy L. Heisel, Toni's high school boyfriend and ex-husband; Jessica Heisel, Toni's daughter; Tim Heisel, Toni's son; Grant Helgeson, Peggy's teammate; Kent Helgeson, Peggy's teammate; Stefan Helgeson, St. Cloud tennis player; Carol Howe-Veenstra, Tech coach; Steve Howe-Veenstra, Peggy's high school classmate; Alicia Jack, Toni's daughter; Mary Jo Kane, founder of the Tucker Center for Research on Girls and Women in Sport at the University of Minnesota; Patrick (David) Lanin, Toni's cross-country running and skiing coach; Gary Lee, Toni's teammate; Don Lee, Toni's teammate; Miles Lord, federal court judge presiding over *Brenden vs. ISD 742*; Priscilla Lord, Judge Lord's daughter; Vida (McQueen) Percy, Toni's teammate; Jeff Peterson, Peggy's teammate; Bill Ritchie, Tech tennis coach; Sam St. Pierre, Toni's brother; Jerry Sales, Tech tennis coach; Sandy and Jim Tool, Brenden family members; Thomas Wexler, attorney representing Peggy and Toni.

Another large cast of supporters helped me with the long process of crafting this book: Jeremy Farmer, the archives technician at the National Archives in Chicago who assisted me in obtaining court transcripts from 1972; the librarians and staff at Minnesota Historical Society, Gale Library, and Hennepin County, who dug out boxes of archives, troubleshot microfilm machines, and copied and ordered articles and books from everywhere; Tech High School Alumni Association Inc., which maintains a school archive; Ronald Sharp, who provided meaningful and constructive feedback on my earliest drafts, giving me the courage to revise, improve, and continue; Jean

Bey, my cousin, who shared her enthusiasm for the book idea and urged Ron to read my manuscript; my neighbors Sue Woodrich and Dave Knoblauch, who eagerly tracked my progress and helped me contact Priscilla Lord; my friends Liz Andress, Jane Blockhus, Diane Brady-Leighton, Teresa Caspar, Becky Halvorson, Sarah Kise, and Bonnie Christensen, who listened to me discuss my writing journey for many years; Laura Weber, who edited and published my article in the Minnesota Historical Society magazine and gave me confidence in the story; Mike and Karel Helgeson, who offered their support and help to navigate the publishing process; Ryan Rodgers, who shared his own publishing experience and helped me connect with the University of Minnesota Press; and Kristian Tvedten, associate editor for the Press, who guided me through revisions, peer reviews, and publishing with insight and encouragement.

Finally, I thank family members who were so supportive: Peggy Brenden, of course, who was nothing but encouraging, helpful, and patient, but also her spouse, Deb Wilson, Sandy Tool, Jim Tool, and Judy Solmonson. I so appreciate the pep club that includes my children—Carl Peaslee, Sarah Peaslee, Emma Peaslee, Tanner Barcus, Sarah Moen, Blake Moen, and my amazing new grandson, Matt.

This book is better (and so is my life) because of my dear husband, Phil Eckhert, who discussed my research, read numerous drafts, and shared meaningful yet always kind feedback. I also appreciate all the delicious meals and unceasing encouragement you provided. You are my superpower.

NOTES

Unless otherwise noted, direct quotations throughout the text are taken from the following interviews conducted by the author. Similarly, remarks made during the trial are reproduced from the official court transcript, *Brenden v. Ind. School Dist.,* No. 4-72-201, D. Minn., April 24–26, 1972.

INTERVIEWS
Paul Bengtson, November 8, 2018.
Peggy Brenden, September 24, 2005.
Peggy Brenden, November 21, 2017.
Jessica Heisel, April 2, 2018.
Tim Heisel, April 16, 2018, Buffalo, Minnesota.
Grant Helgeson, March 21, 2017, Scottsdale, Arizona.
Kent Helgeson, February 22, 2017, St. Joseph, Missouri.
Stefan (Steve) Helgeson, July 2, 2019, Edina, Minnesota.
Mary Jo Kane, April 27, 2021, Minneapolis, Minnesota.
Patrick Lanin, July 13, 2018, Brainerd, Minnesota.
Gary Lee, September 7, 2018.
Miles Lord, March 8, 2006, Minneapolis, Minnesota.
Priscilla Lord, September 14, 2020, Minnetonka, Minnesota.
Jeff Peterson, January 28, 2017.
Bill Ritchie, December 15, 2016, St. Cloud, Minnesota.
Sam St. Pierre, May 11, 2018.
James Tool, November 17, 2005.
Thomas Wexler, November 10, 2005, Minneapolis, Minnesota.

PROLOGUE
1. Established in 1993, the Tucker Center for Research on Girls and Women in Sport is an interdisciplinary research center at the

University of Minnesota that sponsors, promotes, and disseminates research on how sport impacts the lives of girls and women.

2. The case appears in "Eight Significant Cases in the United States District Court for District of Minnesota" in *History of the U.S. District Court,* written and published by the court to celebrate the Constitution's Bicentennial in 1989. Accessed at https://www.mnd.uscourts.gov/sites/mnd/files/3-Significant_Cases.pdf.

3. *Brenden v. Ind. School Dist.* 742, 477 F.2d 1292, 1298 (8th Cir. 1973).

1. THE LETTER

1. Sports journalist Jim McKay uttered this tagline each Saturday afternoon on ABC's *Wide World of Sports.* A montage of video clips and brassy music introduced viewers to the show, which covered the "human drama of athletic competition."

2. The Minnesota Civil Liberties Union is now known as the American Civil Liberties Union of Minnesota (ACLU-MN).

3. This statement is from a July 13, 2018, recorded interview with the author. In order to condense this book's very large list of endnotes, subsequent quotations from author interviews have not been cited individually. See the interviews section at the beginning of these notes for a complete list.

4. Scott A. Herron, "The Girl with a Runner's Heart," *St. Paul Pioneer Press,* November 19, 1972, 14.

5. Started in 1961, the Minnesota Road Runners Club is now known as Run Minnesota.

6. Sarah Barker, "Minnesotan Still Is Devoted to the Sports He Helped Launch for Young Athletes," *Star Tribune,* February 28, 2019.

7. Sarah Barker, "Toni St. Pierre Just Wanted to Run," *Podium Runner,* April 16, 2021.

8. "Mixed Doubles CC Meet Held," *Minneapolis Tribune,* November 9, 1970.

9. Herron, "The Girl with a Runner's Heart."

10. Tom Harmon, "Toni, Lawsuit Seek 'Good Competition,'" *Hopkins Sun,* April 13, 1972, 25.

11. Peggy Brenden, email message to Sheri Brenden, August 19, 2020.

12. "MCLU Eyes Student Voter Eligibility as New Union Forms Here," *St. Cloud Daily Times*, September 8, 1971, 7.

13. Yvonne Hartz case file, October 1971, American Civil Liberties Union of Minnesota Collection, Minnesota History Center, St. Paul, Minnesota.

14. Sylvia Lang, "How Will It Affect Women Here? Women (Lib or No) May Gain Identity," *St. Cloud Daily Times*, April 26, 1972, 34.

15. Mike Knaak, "Can a Girl Be 'One of the Guys'?" *Montage* [St. Cloud Tech student newspaper], November 10, 1971, 3.

16. Joel Rippel, *Minnesota State High School League: One Hundred Years of Memories* (Brooklyn Center: Minnesota State High School League, 2015), 19–20.

17. Rippel, *Minnesota State High School League*, 53.

18. Marian Bemis Johnson and Dorothy E. McIntyre, *Daughters of the Game: The First Era of Minnesota Girls High School Basketball, 1891–1942* (Edina, Minn.: McJohn Publishing LLC, 2005), 74.

19. Johnson and McIntyre, *Daughters of the Game*, 72.

20. Susan K. Cahn, *Coming on Strong: Gender and Sexuality in Twentieth-Century Women's Sport* (New York: The Free Press, 1994), 56 57.

21. Johnson and McIntyre, *Daughters of the Game*, 258.

22. Rippel, *Minnesota State High School League*, 70.

23. Catherine Watson, "Minnesota Girls Compete for Athletic Equality," *Minneapolis Tribune*, March 12, 1972, 1E.

24. Rippel, *Minnesota State High School League*, 60.

25. Dorothy E. McIntyre, "Girls, Boys, and Sports in Minnesota," *Bulletin* [Minnesota State High School League publication] 46, no. 4 (December 1971): 1–3.

26. Karen Blumenthal, *Let Me Play: The Story of Title IX, the Law That Changed the Future of Girls in America* (New York: Atheneum Books for Young Readers, 2005), 31.

27. Margo L. Anderson, "A Legal History and Analysis of Sex Discrimination in Athletics: Mixed Gender Competition, 1970–1987," PhD diss., University of Minnesota, 1989, 117.

28. Rippel, *Minnesota State High School League,* 54.

29. Anne Hamre, "'You Can't Back Out Now,'" *Minnesota Women's Press* 28, no. 6 (June 2012): 10.

30. Rippel, *Minnesota State High School League,* 54.

31. Rippel, *Minnesota State High School League,* 54.

32. Watson, "Minnesota Girls Compete for Athletic Equality," 12E.

33. Howard B. Casmey, Report to the Minnesota State Legislature on the Minnesota State High School League, January 1973, box 6, folder "Minnesota State High School League 1970–1974," Minnesota Department of Education, Commissioner's Office, MHS Collections, 9.

34. "Information" [exhibit from St. Cloud Tech], April 1972, Brenden v. ISD 742 (Civil Action No. 4–72, Civil 201), U.S. District Court, District of Minnesota.

35. Catherine Watson, "Girls' Sports—How Equal Is 'Separate'?" *Minneapolis Tribune,* March 19, 1972, 8E–9E.

36. Marian Rengel and Carol Rundquist, "Girls and Hockey Bust Budget," *Montage* 2, no. 8 (May 24, 1972): 5.

37. Exhibit E, "St. Cloud Tech High School Tennis Schedule 1972," April 1972, Brenden v. ISD 742 (Civil Action No. 4–72, Civil 201), U.S. District Court, District of Minnesota; 1972 Tennis score books maintained by St. Cloud Tech coaches.

38. Rippel, *Minnesota State High School League,* 77.

39. John J. Dominik Jr., *Three Towns into One City* (St. Cloud Area Bicentennial Commission, 1978), 66.

40. Gertrude B. Gove, *A Century of Progress: A History of the St. Cloud, Minnesota Public Schools,* 1958.

2. KILL 'EM WITH COOL

1. Sarah K. Fields, *Female Gladiators: Gender, Law, and Contact Sport in America* (Urbana–Champaign: University of Illinois Press, 2008), 14.

2. Last I checked, that little trophy is still under the sink in Peggy's bathroom. When she cleared out nearly all the bowls, platters, and plaques from her tennis career, she carefully held on to her first trophy.

3. COURT STRATEGY

1. Peggy Brenden case file, November 20, 1971, American Civil Liberties Union of Minnesota Collection, Minnesota History Center, St. Paul, Minnesota.

2. MCLU Board of Directors Meeting #3, Saturday, April 22, 1972 Minutes, Minnesota History Center, St. Paul, Minnesota.

3. Dick Hewetson, *History of the Gay Movement in Minnesota and the Role of the Minnesota Civil Liberties Union* (Minneapolis: Dr. Matthew Stark and Friends of the Bill of Rights Foundation, 2013), 5.

4. C-2072 St. Pierre, Marie v. Independent School District No. 274 and Minnesota State High School League, American Civil Liberties Union of Minnesota records, Minnesota History Center, St. Paul, Minnesota.

5. Sylvia Lang, "Tech Senior Might Set Precedent, Wants Spot on Varsity Tennis Team," *St. Cloud Daily Times*, April 12, 1972, 32.

6. Anderson, "Legal History and Analysis," 141.

7. UPI, "Peggy Brenden Sues St. Cloud District to Play High School Sports," *St. Cloud Daily Times*, April 6, 1972, 1; Sylvia Lang, "Tech Senior Might Set Precedent, Wants Spot on Varsity Tennis Team," *St. Cloud Daily Times*, April 12, 1972, 32; Tom Harmon, "Toni, Lawsuit Seek 'Good Competition,'" *Hopkins Sun*, April 13, 1972, 25; Gwenyth Jones, "2 Girls Sue State Prep League," *Minneapolis Star*, April 6, 1972, 1D; Bob Protzman, "Suit Filed to Place Girls on Boys' Athletic Teams," *St. Paul Dispatch*, April 5, 1972, 35.

8. "St. Cloud May Back Girl Netter," April 13, 1972, *Minneapolis Star*, 40.

9. "District 742 against Girl on Boys' Team," *St. Cloud Daily Times*, April 24, 1972, 1.

10. Roberta Walburn, *Miles Lord: The Maverick Judge Who Brought Corporate America to Justice* (Minneapolis: University of Minnesota Press, 2017), 51, 139.

11. Walburn, *Miles Lord*, 222.

12. Mark Streed, "Miles Lord: A Warrior Fighting for Justice," *Minnesota Trial*, Summer 2009, 38.

13. Streed, "Miles Lord," 38.

14. Mark D. Streed, "Miles Lord: A Warrior Fighting for Justice," *Minnesota Trial,* Summer 2009, 38.

15. Dave Orrick and Will Ashenbacher, "Miles Lord, 'Pivotal' Federal Judge Who Helped Shape MN and U.S. Policies, Dies at 97," *Pioneer Press,* December 10, 2016, http://www.twincities.com /2016/12/10/miles-lord-pivotal-federal-judge-who-helped-shape-mn -and-u-s-policies-dies-at-97.

16. Orrick and Ashenbacher, "Miles Lord."

17. Judge Miles Lord, "Notes from 11/12/1985," provided by the Lord family.

18. Bernhard LeVander, *Call Me Pete: Memoir of a Minnesota Man,* ed. Grant Dawson (Reno: Dawson Creative Ltd. Effort, 2006), unpaginated.

19. Brown v. Wells, 181 N.W.2d 708 (1970).

20. Lord, "Notes from 11/12/1985."

21. LeVander, *Call Me Pete.*

22. Lord, "Notes from 11/12/1985."

23. Rippel, *Minnesota State High School League,* 68.

24. Miles Lord funeral, comments by Priscilla Lord Faris, Mount Calvary Lutheran Church, Excelsior, Minnesota, January 12, 2017.

25. Transcript, vol. I, Brenden v ISD 742, p. 19, April 24, 1972.

26. "Tigers, Eagles Post Victories," *St. Cloud Daily Times,* April 18, 1972, 19.

27. "St. Cloud may back girl netter," *Minneapolis Star,* April 13, 1972, 40.

28. Affidavit of Dorothy E. McIntyre, Brenden v. ISD 742, filed April 21, 1972, 2–4.

29. Complaint, Brenden v. ISD 742, filed April 5, 1972, 3.

30. Larry Millett, "Girls Sports Plan OKd Here," *St. Cloud Daily Times,* April 21, 1972, 3.

31. "2 Girls to Play Tennis on Boys Team," *Minneapolis Star,* April 18, 1972, 2D.

32. Transcript, vol. 1, Brenden v. ISD 742, p. 17, April 24, 1972. Also referenced in Tech Tennis team scorebook.

33. Jim Holden, *Tennis in the Northland* (Edina, Minn.: Beaver's Pond Press, 2008), 318–19.

34. "Brenden Law Suit Ends But Not Forever," *Montage*, May 24, 1972, 11.

35. C. Brettschneider, ed., *Decisions and Dissents of Justice Ruth Bader Ginsburg: A Selection* (New York: Penguin Books, 2020), 4–5 [ebook edition].

36. Brettschneider, *Decisions and Dissents,* xxv, xxviii.

37. Justice Ruth Bader Ginsburg, Gillian Metzger, and Abbe R. Gluck, "A Conversation with Justice Ruth Bader Ginsburg," 2013, Faculty Scholarship Series, Paper 4905, Lillian Goldman Law Library, Yale University, accessed August 9, 2017, http://hdl.handle.net/20.500.13051/4436.

38. Brettschneider, *Decisions and Dissents,* 9.

39. "Tribute: The Legacy of Ruth Bader and WRP Staff," American Civil Liberties Union, accessed August 9, 2017, https://www.aclu.org/other/tribute-legacy-ruth-bader-ginsburg-and-wrp-staff.

40. Dorothy Stetson and Dorothy E. McBride, *Women's Rights in the U.S.A.: Policy Debates and Gender Roles* (New York: Garland Publishing, 1997), 34.

41. Lesley Oelsner, "Teaneck Girl Sues to Join High School Tennis Team," *New York Times,* February 1, 1972, 33.

42. Transcript, vol. II, Brenden v. ISD 742, April 25, 1972, 238.

43. Sarah K. Fields, *Female Gladiators: Gender, Law, and Contact Sport in America* (Urbana–Champaign: University of Illinois Press, 2008), 5.

44. 118 Cong. Rec. 5808 (February 28, 1972).

45. Jaime Schultz, *Qualifying Times: Points of Change in U.S. Women's Sport* (Urbana–Champaign: University of Illinois Press, 2014), 127–128. Schultz quotes from the 1973 *Sports Illustrated* article.

46. Ginny Gilder, *Course Correction: A Story of Rowing and Resilience in the Wake of Title IX* (Boston: Beacon Press, 2015), 46.

47. Susan Ware, *Game, Set, Match* (Chapel Hill: University of North Carolina Press, 2011), 24–33.

48. Bil Gilbert and Nancy Williamson, "Sport Is Unfair to Women," *Sports Illustrated,* May 28, 1973, 92.

49. Susan K. Cahn, *Coming On Strong: Gender and Sexuality in*

Twentieth-Century Women's Sport (New York: The Free Press, 1994), 252.

4. TAKING THE STAND

1. Transcripts, Brenden v. ISD 742 (4-72 Civil 201), April 24–26, 1972. Filed in U.S. District Court, District of Minnesota. All testimony reproduced in these chapters is from these court transcripts.

2. The court transcript misspells Antoinette St. Pierre's name "Tony." I have silently corrected it to "Toni" throughout.

3. Patrick O'Regan, "Toni St. Pierre, a Runner Who Made a Difference," *RunMinnesota* 9, no. 1 (January/February 2010), 18.

4. Murrae N. Freng, Defendant Minnesota State High School League Answers to Interrogatories, p. 1, April 24, 1972.

5. "District 742 against Girl on Boys' Team," 1.

5. EDUCATORS AND EXPERTS

1. "Miss Brenden to 'Suit' Up with Boys?" *St. Cloud Daily Times,* April 25, 1972, 1; "Boys to Dominate Teams If Girls Are Eligible— Freng," *Minneapolis Star,* April 25, 1972, 1. The latter story was from the *Star's* wire services.

2. "Court Hears Plea for Girls on Boys' Teams," April 25, 1972, *Minneapolis Tribune,* 1B.

3. Marg Zack, "St. Paul Girl Ready to Swim, Beached by Rules," December 14, 1971, *Minneapolis Tribune,* 1B; Bonnie Watkins and Nina Rothchild, *In the Company of Women: Voices from the Women's Movement* (St. Paul: Minnesota Historical Society Press, 1996), 122–23.

4. Bob Schranck, "Girls Getting Pretty Darn Good in Track," *Minneapolis Star,* May 15, 1971, 16A.

6. IN CLOSING

1. UPI, "Physiology May Defeat Girls," *St. Cloud Daily Times,* April 26, 1972, 1.

2. Bob Lundergaard, "Witnesses Back League Ban on Girls," *Minneapolis Tribune,* April 26, 1972, 4B.

3. Bob Schranck. "Court Decision Key to Girls' Athletic Future," *Minneapolis Star,* April 26, 1972, 7D.

4. "Tech Netmen Still Unbeaten," *St. Cloud Daily Times,* April 26, 1972, 41.

5. Herron, "Girl with a Runner's Heart," 14.

6. Transcript, vol. III, Brenden v. ISD 742, April 26, 1972, 319–20, 323.

7. Freng did not actually note that he was talking about only the boys' track team. He simply referred to "track."

8. Bob Lundergaard, "Girl Athlete Injuries Called Problem," *Minneapolis Tribune,* April 27, 1972, 16B.

9. Transcript, vol. III, Brenden v. ISD 742, April 25, 1972, 336–337; David Miller, "Board Assumes 'Split' Stance on Prohibition of Girls' Vying in Boys' Sports," *Hopkins Sun,* April 27, 1972, 1.

10. Lundergaard, "Girl Athlete Injuries Called Problem," 16B.

7. DECISION

1. Reed v. Nebraska School Activities Assn., 341 F.Supp. 258, 260 (D. Neb. 1972).

2. Morris v. Michigan State Board of Education, 472 F.2d 1207 (E.D. Mich. 1972).

3. Gene Sperling, "The Battle for Title IX and the Opportunities It Created," Barack Obama White House archives, June 23, 2012, accessed August 9, 2017. https://obamawhitehouse.archives.gov /blog/2012/06/23/battle-title-ix-and-opportunities-it-created.

4. Mitchell v. Louisiana High School Athletic Assn., 430 F.2d 1155.

5. 342 F. Supp. 1224, 1234.

6. 342 F. Supp. 1224, 1229.

7. 342 F. Supp. 1224, 1230.

8. 342 F. Supp. 1224, 1231–32.

9. *History for the District Court for the District of Minnesota,* 26.

10. 342 F. Supp. 1224, 1233–34.

8. VIOLATION OF THE FOURTEENTH AMENDMENT

1. Associated Press, "MSHSL to Appeal Girls' Court Ruling," *Fergus Falls Daily Journal,* May 6, 1972, 5.

2. "MSHSL to Appeal Girls' Court Ruling," 5.

3. Marvin Helling, "Women's Rights in Athletics," *Women's*

Athletics: Coping with Controversy, ed. Barbara J. Hoepner (from 1973 American Association for Health, Physical Education, and Recreation Convention, Minneapolis, Minnesota), 23, accessed May 16, 2017. https://files.eric.ed.gov/fulltext/ED092550.pdf.

4. From Peggy Brenden's scrapbook.

5. Mike Knaak and Richard Boltuck, "'Tennis Anyone?'—Courts Say Maybe," *Montage,* May 24, 1972, 4.

6. "Brenden Law Suit Ends But Not Forever," *Montage,* May 24, 1972, 11.

7. Editorial board, "Equality in Sports," *Minneapolis Star,* May 8, 1972.

8. Jim Wells, "Girls Can Compete, Schools Expect No Snags," *St Paul Pioneer Press,* May 2, 1972.

9. Pat Thompson, "Girls Can Play Boys' Sports But . . ." *Fergus Falls Daily Journal,* May 4, 1972, 11.

10. Knaak and Boltuck, "'Tennis Anyone?'" 4.

11. Wells, "Girls Can Compete."

12. David Miller, "How the Ladies Won It Vying in Boys' Sports," *Hopkins Sun,* April 27, 1972, 1.

13. David Miller, "Girls' Sports Get Go-Ahead; Boys' Athletics Take Lumps," *Hopkins Sun,* June 29, 1972, 1.

14. Miller, "Girls' Sports Get Go-Ahead," 1.

15. Marian Rengel and Carol Rundquist, "Girls and Hockey Bust Budget," *Montage,* May 24, 1972, 5.

9. PEGGY'S MATCH

1. UPI, "Court Rules City Girl May Compete with Boys," *St. Cloud Daily Times,* May 1, 1972, 1.

2. John J. Dominik, *St. Cloud: The Triplet City* (Woodland Hills, Calif.: Windsor Publications, 1983), 160.

3. Lang, "Tech Senior Might Set Precedent," 32.

4. Bob Schranck, "Girl Tennis Player 'No. 3 Man,'" *Minneapolis Star,* May 5, 1972, 11B.

5. Schranck, "Girl Tennis Player 'No. 3 Man,'" 11B.

6. Jim Wells, "Peggy Bows in Debut; 'I Choked,' She Says," *St. Paul Pioneer Press,* May 7, 1972, 5.

7. Thompson, "Girls Can Play," 11.

8. Wells, "Peggy Bows in Debut," 5.

9. "Edina Tops Ratings in Prep Tennis," *Minneapolis Tribune,* May 9, 1972, 4C.

10. "History Is Made in Coon Rapids," *Coon Rapids Herald,* May 12, 1972, 14.

11. Thompson, "Girls Can Play," 11.

12. "History Is Made at Coon Rapids," 14.

13. "History Is Made at Coon Rapids," 14.

14. Wells, "Peggy Bows in Debut," 5.

15. "Girl Prep Enters Boys' Area, Loses," *Minneapolis Tribune,* May 7, 1972.

16. Schranck, "Girl Tennis Player 'No. 3 Man,'" 11B.

17. John Dietz, "Tennis Team 7–2 after Win, Loss," *Sherburne County Star News,* May 11, 1972, 5.

18. "Netmen Rebound 3–2 over Wadena," *Brainerd Daily Dispatch,* May 16, 1972, 13.

19. "Tech Netters Trip Eagles," *St. Cloud Daily Times,* May 16, 1972, 18.

20. "Tigers Nudge Apollo Netmen," *St. Cloud Daily Times,* April 29, 1972, 10.

21. Jim Holden, *Tennis in the Northland* (Edina, Minn.: Beaver's Pond Press, 2008), 317.

22. "Tigers Win Net Title," *St. Cloud Daily Times,* May 26, 1972.

23. Holden, *Tennis in the Northland,* 266.

24. Holden, *Tennis in the Northland,* 61.

10. TONI'S RACE

1. Rob Held, "International Falls, WBL Pace Girls State Meet," *St. Cloud Daily Times,* May 30, 1971, 27. The *St. Cloud Daily Times* took three days to publish its coverage of the first-ever girls' state high school athletic competition, which was hosted in town. Perhaps that was because neither St. Cloud Tech nor Apollo scored any team points, or perhaps it is because the newspaper did not have a reporter assigned to the girls' sports beat.

2. Bruce Brothers, "High School Sports," *Minneapolis Tribune,* May 30, 1972, 27.

3. In studies of media sports coverage since 1989, Cheryl Cooky and Michael A. Messner found that female athleticism is often trivialized, and women's sports are portrayed as unimportant or uninteresting. Michael A. Messner, "The Gender of Sports Media," in *No Slam Dunk: Gender, Sport, and the Unevenness of Social Change* (New Brunswick, N.J.: Rutgers University Press, 2018), 217, 227–28.

4. Kathrine Switzer, "First Woman's Strides in Boston Still Echoing," *New York Times,* April 15, 2007.

5. "Marathon Women," Morning Edition, National Public Radio, April 15, 2002, https://www.npr.org/templates/story/story.php?storyId=1141740.

6. Official program, Minnesota State High School League 50th Annual High School Track and Field Meet (June 10, 1972, Macalester College, St. Paul, Minnesota).

7. Held, "International Falls, WBL Pace Girls State Meet," 27.

8. Brian Anderson, "Proud Parents Cheer for Daughters in First Girls' Track Meet in 30 Years," *Minneapolis Tribune,* May 28, 1972, 6B.

9. Bob Schranck, "Girls Getting Pretty Darn Good in Track," *Minneapolis Star,* May 15, 1971, 16A.

10. Schranck, "Girls Getting Pretty Darn Good in Track," 16A.

11. O'Regan, "Toni St Pierre," 18.

12. O'Regan, "Toni St Pierre," 18.

13. James Parson, "Girl Runner Hits New Block in Bid 'to Run with Guys,'" *Minneapolis Tribune,* October 4, 1972, 1A.

14. Parson, "Girl Runner Hits New Block," 1A.

15. "Attention Called to Rule Changes," *Bulletin* XLVII, no. 1 (August 1972): 5.

16. Parson, "Girl Runner Hits New Block," 8A.

17. Parson, "Girl Runner Hits New Block," 8A.

18. Parson, "Girl Runner Hits New Block," 8A.

19. Herron, "Girl with a Runner's Heart," 13.

20. Parson, "Girl Runner Hits New Block," 8A.

21. John Sherman, Sports column, *Hopkins Sailor,* October 26, 1972, 11.

22. John Sherman, "Ike Cross Country Skiers," *Hopkins Sun,* February 1, 1973, 7.

23. "Toni Travels with US Team," *Hopkins Sun,* February 15, 1973, 13.

24. "Woman Runner Tries Out for St. John's Squad," *Minneapolis Star,* December 4, 1973, 2D.

11. "THE COURTS FORCED THIS ON US"

1. "Women's Cases Taken by MCLU," December 1973, box 20, ACLU-MN, Minnesota Historical Society.

2. "Suit on Girls' Ban Threatened," *Minneapolis Star,* October 25, 1972, 3D.

3. "On Anoka Swim Team, Bid by Two Girls Rejected," *Minneapolis Star,* October 27, 1972, 12B.

4. "Judge Allows Edina Girl to Join Ski Team," *Minneapolis Tribune,* January 24, 1973, 2B.

5. "First Meeting of the Representative Assembly," *Bulletin* XLVII, no. 5 (December 1972): A-11.

6. Robert C. Tucker, clerk to U.S. Court of Appeals 8th Circuit judges, September 28, 1972, "Case No. 72–1287 Torbin H. Brenden, etc., et al v. Minnesota State High School League," box 25, Gerald W. Heaney Papers, Minnesota Historical Society (hereafter "Case No. 72–1287").

7. Amicus brief filed by Nebraska State School Board Association, August 23, 1972, Case No. 72–1287.

8. Oral argument notes, January 8, 1973, Case No. 72–1287.

9. Bonnie J. Morris and D-M Withers, *The Feminist Revolution: The Struggle for Women's Liberation* (London: Elephant Publishing Company, 2018), 46–47.

10. Morris and Withers, 46–47.

11. Stanford Lehmberg and Ann M. Pflaum, *The University of Minnesota, 1945–2000* (Minneapolis: University of Minnesota Press, 2001), 172–73.

12. Lehmberg and Pflaum, *University of Minnesota,* 172–73.

13. Jaime Schultz, *Qualifying Times: Points of Change in U.S. Women's Sport* (Urbana–Champaign: University of Illinois Press, 2014), 128.

14. Schultz, *Qualifying Times,* 131.

15. Ellen J. Staurowsky, "Title IX and College Sport: The Long Painful Path to Compliance and Reform," *Marquette Sports Law Review* 14, no. 1 (Fall 2003): 100–102.

16. Paul M. Anderson, "Title IX at Forty: An Introduction and Historical Review of Forty Legal Developments That Shaped Gender Equity Law," *Marquette Sports Law Review* 329 (2012): 22.

17. Anderson, "Title IX at Forty."

18. Andrew Keh, "A Girl Wanted to Try Out for Boys' Tennis. Ginsburg Helped Make It Happen," *New York Times,* September 23, 2020 (updated September 26, 2020). https://www.nytimes.com /2020/09/23/sports/tennis/ruth-bader-ginsburg-tennis.html.

19. *Brenden v. Ind. School Dist.* 742, 477 F.2d 1292 (8th Cir. 1973).

20. Bruce Brothers, "Ruling Opens Prep Doors to Girl Athletes," *Minneapolis Tribune,* April 20, 1973, 1C.

21. Bob Schranck, "Girls in Sport Okd," *Minneapolis Star,* April 20, 1973, 11B.

22. "Hopkins Eisenhower High School Use of Ineligible Players," *Bulletin* XLVIII, no. 1 (August 1973): 15.

23. Linda Kohl, "Sports Ruling Disputed," *St. Paul Dispatch,* May 19, 1973, 28.

24. Bruce Brothers, "Football Opened to Prep Girls," *Minneapolis Tribune,* April 28, 1973, 1B.

25. Bruce Brothers, high school sports column, *Minneapolis Tribune,* May 1, 1973, 3C.

26. John Sherman, "MSHSL Goes off Deep End, and So May Girls' Sports," *Hopkins Sun,* May 17, 1973.

27. Rippel, *100 Years of Memories,* 61, 54; Diane LeBlanc and Allys Swanson, *Playing for Equality: Oral Histories of Women Leaders in the Early Years of Title IX* (Jefferson, N.C.: McFarland and Company, Inc., 2016), 105.

28. Joe Soucheray, "'I've Been Called a Jockette,'" *Minneapolis Tribune Picture Magazine,* December 9, 1973, 44.

29. Holden, *Tennis in the Northland,* 318–22.

30. Eileen McDonagh and Laura Pappano, *Playing with the Boys: Why Separate Is Not Equal in Sports* (New York: Oxford University Press, 2007), 32.

31. Herbert Warren Wind, *Game, Set, and Match: The Tennis Boom of the 1960s and 70s* (New York: E. P. Dutton, 1979), 118.

32. Billie Jean King with Cynthia Starr, *We Have Come a Long Way: The Story of Women's Tennis* (New York: McGraw-Hill, 1988), 146.

12. STAND UP

1. Nancy Lough, "Proof in the Data: New Model Emerging for Women's Sport," *Sports Business Journal,* November 2, 2020. https://www.sportsbusinessjournal.com/Journal/Issues/2020/11/02/Opinion/Lough.aspx.

2. Messner and Cooky, *No Slam Dunk,* 228.

3. "NCAA External Gender Equity Review: Phase I, Basketball Championships," Kaplan Hecker & Fink LLP. https://kaplanhecker.app.box.com/s/xc1v5gjnmk4ndku1s2n2n1net4fwczeh.

4. Joan Steiniger, *Stand Up and Shout Out: Women's Fight for Equal Pay, Equal Rights, and Equal Opportunities in Sports* (Lanham: Rowman and Littlefield, 2020), 70.

5. Janet S. Fink, "Hiding in Plain Sight: The Embedded Nature of Sexism in Sport," *Journal of Sport Management* 30, no. 1 (2016): 4. https://doi.org/10.1123/jsm.2015-0278.

6. Joshua A. Senne, "Examination of Gender Equity and Female Participation in Sport," *Sport Journal* 19 (February 26, 2016). https://thesportjournal.org/article/examination-of-gender-equity-and-female-participation-in-sport; E. J. Staurowsky et al., *Chasing Equity: The Triumphs, Challenges, and Opportunities in Sports for Girls and Women* (New York: Women's Sports Foundation, 2020). https://www.womenssportsfoundation.org/wp-content/uploads/2020/01/Chasing-Equity-Full-Report-Web.pdf.

7. Jenna Ashendouek, "Title IX: A Milestone for Women in

Sports, but Unfulfilled Promise for Black Women," *Ms.*, July 14, 2020. https://msmagazine.com/2020/07/14/title-ix-a-milestone -for-women-in-sports-but-unfulfilled-promise-for-black-women.

8. O'Regan, "Toni St. Pierre," 19.

FURTHER READING

Blumenthal, Karen. *Let Me Play: The Story of Title IX, the Law That Changed the Future of Girls in America*. New York: Atheneum Books for Young Readers, 2005.

Cahn, Susan K. *Coming on Strong: Gender and Sexuality in Twentieth-Century Women's Sport*. New York: The Free Press, 1994.

Chocano, Carina. *You Play the Girl: On Playboy Bunnies, Stepford Wives, Train Wrecks, and Other Mixed Messages*. Boston: Houghton Mifflin Harcourt, 2017.

Fields, Sarah K. *Female Gladiators: Gender, Law, and Contact Sport in America*. Urbana–Champaign: University of Illinois Press, 2008.

Heywood, Leslie. *Pretty Good for a Girl: An Athlete's Story*. Minneapolis: University of Minnesota Press, 2000.

Holden, Jim. *Tennis in the Northland*. Edina, Minn.: Beaver's Pond Press, 2008.

Johnson, Marian Bemis, and Dorothy E. McIntyre. *Daughters of the Game: The First Era of Minnesota Girls High School Basketball, 1891–1942*. Edina, Minn.: McJohn Publishing LLC, 2005.

King, Billie Jean, with Cynthia Starr. *We Have Come a Long Way: The Story of Women's Tennis*. New York: McGraw-Hill, 1988.

McDonagh, Eileen, and Laura Pappano. *Playing with the Boys: Why Separate Is Not Equal in Sports*. New York: Oxford University Press, 2007.

Messner, Michael A., and Cheryl Cooky. *No Slam Dunk: Gender, Sport, and the Unevenness of Social Change,* Critical Issues in Sport and Society. New Brunswick: Rutgers University Press, 2018.

Ridder, Kathleen C., editor. *Leveling the Playing Field: Stories by Minnesota Women in Sports*. St. Cloud: North Star Press, 2005.

Rippel, Joel. *Minnesota State High School League: One Hundred Years of Memories.* Brooklyn Center: Minnesota State High School League, 2015.

Schultz, Jaime. *Qualifying Times: Points of Change in U.S. Women's Sport.* Urbana–Champaign: University of Illinois Press, 2014.

Steidinger, Joan. *Stand Up and Shout Out: Women's Fight for Equal Pay, Equal Rights, and Equal Opportunities in Sports.* Lanham, Md.: Rowman and Littlefield, 2020.

Walburn, Roberta. *Miles Lord: The Maverick Judge Who Brought Corporate America to Justice.* Minneapolis: University of Minnesota Press, 2017.

Ware, Susan. *Game, Set, Match: Billie Jean King and the Revolution in Women's Sports.* Chapel Hill: University of North Carolina Press, 2011.

SHERI BRENDEN is a former research librarian for two of Minnesota's largest law firms. She has also worked as a writer, editor, and newspaper reporter.